A TROUT
FISHERMAN'S
SOUL

TONY DINCAU

authorHOUSE®

AuthorHouse™
1663 Liberty Drive
Bloomington, IN 47403
www.authorhouse.com
Phone: 833-262-8899

Published by AuthorHouse 02/10/2021

ISBN: 978-1-6655-1489-7 (sc)
ISBN: 978-1-6655-1505-4 (e)

Library of Congress Control Number: 2021901437

Contents

"A Mother's Wish"

The front cover displays a touching watercolor painting by the late Linda Dincau, depicting any one of her three sons on a trout stream. Little did she know that her love of family, nature, and art would one day grace the outside of a book.

Dedication

For my grandfather who made an everlasting impression, for my father who continued our traditions, and for my mother who blessed our every adventure.

Acknowledgements

A number of people guided me during the three years it took to produce this book. I am indebted to Lana Henry for her editing skills and writing pointers. Angela Lalande helped me set the book's frame while providing a thorough review. Peggy Pitre, Dominik Ellena, and Trevor Casper provided insightful reviews that greatly improved the final product. National Book Award winning author Pete Hetherington offered very helpful advice after his read, which I incorporated with gratitude. Sheila Zepernick gave me some great feedback that enhanced the manuscript.

I tapped the memories of my family members to sharpen my recollection of our trips. I greatly appreciate their support and enthusiasm during the entire writing process, including our daughter Amanda who meticulously drew a brook trout in my brother hands. My wife Snez, my final reader, deserves thanks for her patience while I spent countless hours writing and rewriting.

Preface

The river has always been a teacher to me, complimenting my forefather's mentoring ways as we coursed its meandering flow. But as I have aged, I've become less interested in how to fish and more interested in why I'm still going. Perhaps that's a natural progression for outdoor-oriented folks, where immersion in nature teaches of things around us, and then years later teaches of things within us.

That's what a trout stream offers, it's a wholesome place where family and friends can connect on a different level, a pure level, where you can unwind and relax. Out there the laughs are heartier, the senses are sharper, and the memories are stronger. When you've finished your day playing among the water and rocks, when you've lost all track of time, you reflect for a minute and know that you've been touched. And you are drawn to go back, because it makes you a better person.

This memoir ushers the reader into the wilds where you can walk with us as we practice our craft and ponder nature's ways. Perhaps you'll set foot into your own sanctuary, and learn a little bit more about yourself.

A Trout Fisherman's Soul

What triggers you to soul search, and where does it take you? Do you embrace it and grow? A life-threatening blood clot behind my left knee in May 2012 shook me and caused a grassroots reflection on my life's path. It took me, unexpectedly, to a trout stream rich with sixty years and four generations of family history, where I grew as a person and learned the value of positive role models.

I live with passion. I love family, so I became a family man. I am fascinated with the earth, so I became a geologist. I enjoy the outdoors, so I became a sportsman. I also admire traditions, especially those that involve my family and the outdoors. This mixture of traits had created a deep imprint within me, one that I was destined to explore.

Undoubtedly, my health scare jump-started some soul searching. It's a shame that it often takes a life-alerting situation to learn more about ourselves. However, I wasn't sure what to make of it all. Was I just stumbling over the age-old question, "What is the meaning of life?" Well, not quite, because I was looking for something more personal, yet common to everyone. Perhaps it's not about life's meaning, but more about what's been meaningful in my life. In other words, what experiences have shaped me to become who I am? Can I recognize the goodness and carry it forward? It was time to answer those questions for myself.

As I dug deeper, I realized that some of my most fulfilling times occurred at the Flag River in northern Wisconsin, where my love of family traditions, nature, and a purposeful sport weaved together. My feelings run deep in that neck of the woods because four generations of my family have fished that trout stream. I started fishing at eight years old under the guidance of my father and late grandfather. Trout fishing was Gramps' passion and he practiced his craft with a style and flair that was infectious; the Flag River remained a part of his life until his final days. My father, a seasoned successor, continued our storied trips for several years after Gramps' departure. He eventually stopped fishing as his interest dwindled with age.

Although I was only fourteen when Gramps passed away, I had enough trips under my belt to be branded a trout fisherman for life. As I aged and my passion for the sport grew, I realized the importance of continuing our family ways with my younger brothers and our children. Someone needed to tell the stories of our forefather's adventures and paint the scenes of our family's art. Someone needed to pass the torch, and that someone was me.

So, for reasons beyond the catch, our family stream continues to draw me back. It's a mystery of sorts, this yearning I feel. Have you ever been drawn to a personal refuge with family history, where you smile while nearly crying, where you grow old while living young, where your dreams can still be real?

Although I found such a place, I'm intrigued with my mystical tie to the Flag. There was something deep and connective about our family experiences that needed uncovering, and as a fact-finding geologist, I was driven to understand the reasons. As a passionate human, I was determined to understand my feelings.

1

One Man's Tale

I lie stretched out in my favorite recliner contemplating these very thoughts. An early evening sun winks through our transom windows, while in the distant background muffled sounds from my neighbor's lawnmower remind me of similar summer settings back in my youth.

In the next room, my wife brings life to the kitchen as she prepares for dinner. Our three children, by some small miracle, are all home at the same time. It's not often that our son of twenty years and our sixteen- and eighteen-year-old daughters are all together. I look forward to a full family dinner later that evening.

I'm trying to fight off a persistent nap, but after forty-eight years on this planet, the ole body develops a mind of its own. The television suddenly carries a familiar tune, bringing a half-asleep grin to my face. A rerun of *Gunsmoke*, one of my late grandfathers' favorite shows, is gracing my screen. I need not open my eyes, for the music itself carries me back to younger years when I lay in bed at my grandparent's house the night before our annual trout fishing and camping trip to the Flag River. It's funny how a melody can transport a person's mind to a different place and time. In a matter of seconds, my mind recreates a comforting scene from back in my youth.

"Sweet dreams," my grandmother said, as she tucked me into bed before our trip. I rested within a halo of dim light and breathed in the smells of my Italian grandparents' house, which was a distinctive combination of homemade pasta sauce and fresh apple pie, with an overtone of mothballs of all things. The penetrating sounds of *Gunsmoke* galloped from Gramps' living room television and echoed down the hallway and into my room. My tummy digested a late night snack of crunchy Bugles, a can of Dr. Pepper, and a handful of M&M's I had snatched from Grandma's hallway candy dish.

The night before our fishing trip was a big one for me. It ranked right up there with the night before my birthday and the night before Christmas. I gladly fell asleep with visions of stream trout dancing through my head.

The next morning I was greeted to a full box of sugary Corn Pops, which was a treat because we rarely had "sugar" cereal at my parent's house. Grandma's old tin cereal bowls somehow made the milk colder and the Corn Pops tastier. I dug into the bowl of goodies like there was no tomorrow, while Gramps and Grandma finished packing for our two day fishing trip.

Even now as an adult those times are still special, for why else would I remember such detail from nearly forty years ago? Those early trout fishing trips led to many others, as one trip after another plays through my mind. There are more with my grandpa, dad, uncle, and even my wife. Many trips were shared with friends, and a bunch more were shared with my brothers, son, and nephew.

The highlight reel of those fishing adventures causes me to reflect on the present day. With eyes closed, the Flag River nearly flows through my living room. With eyes open, it seems a million miles away. My eyes stay shut for now.

It still amuses me that I live so unexpectedly far from where I was raised. My mind sifts through the comforting times in my original home. My first twenty-four years were spent in the small railroad town of Proctor, Minnesota, which snuggles beside Duluth and overlooks Lake Superior. Family and friends encircled me. I soaked up the northland's boundless outdoors with an insatiable desire. I not only enjoyed the land through outdoor activities, but as a budding geologist, I enjoyed studying it to the point of getting a college degree. Ironically, while my passionate interest in exploring the earth drew me closer to my homeland, it ultimately led me away from where I was attached. Such was my fate, I guess.

A career path in geology led me to Lafayette, Louisiana, and twenty-four years of living in Cajun country. My wife and I started a new branch of the family tree deep in the South. We met a new batch of friends, and I was exposed to the outdoors, southern style. I was introduced to a new section of earth to study, much to my delight. Now, the notion to leave this area seems absurd, as it has become a home away from home. What cards will my Maker deal this time?

I have no regrets about relocating, just contemplations.

My wife and I married up North, but our children were born and raised down South. The contrast between the two areas is as stark as a fleck of black pepper among grains of salt.

There's the cold punch of a blizzard versus the hot, humid blow of a hurricane. Thirty below with dry air is as unpleasant as 100 above with moist air. One person goes ice fishing while another goes crabbing. Accordions push a lively polka while a fiddle and squeezebox play for Cajun dancers. Meat and potatoes rule the North but spicy Cajun seafood is king down South. A link of bratwurst welcomes over a link of boudin. In the North, animals eat crayfish; in the South, people eat crawfish. Ten thousand freshwater lakes relate to the vastness of the salty Gulf. Where moose stand in peat bogs, alligators swim in cypress swamps. A northern red maple dressed in brilliant autumn colors compares to the haunting beauty of a southern live oak draped in Spanish moss. Someone says "Eh?" while another says "Who Dat?" And in fun, Oivo and Toivo laughers meet their match with Boudreaux and Thibodeaux jokes.

Sometimes the special features of an area hit home during moments of peace and tranquility, tattooing a scene in one's mind.

Such is the case when the outdoors calls, and a man sets out alone. His canoe skims across a clear lake in search of walleyes. One billion-year-old rocks cradle the calm body of water. The haunting yodel of a loon bounces off rimming trees and fills his ears. Evergreen tops serrate the northland's skyline. A warm feeling wells inside the man as cool air licks his cheeks. He stops his stroke. He glides and wonders.

The same man in a pirogue skims across the marsh in search of redfish. Ten thousand-year-old sediments gently rock the water above. The prehistoric figure of a brown pelican floats overhead and sends an eerie chill through his body. Waves of marsh grasses march southward and blend into the Gulf's horizon. A cool feeling grows inside the man as warm air greets his cheeks. He stops his stroke. He glides and wonders.

Fortunate is the person who not only spins a tale, but also lives the tale that is spun. I am that fortunate person.

While each land is distinctive, there is a common tie between the peoples as families and friends share their lives together along many fronts, forming the strongest of bonds. They celebrate their heritage and culture through countless festivals, parties, and reunions. My experience with people has taught me that if location-based differences are melted away, we are all quite the same.

Nature also draws people together; its beauty calls to the human soul. Its preservation often acts as glue that binds humans as one. Most folks realize that their homegrown surroundings often define them, as the landscape shapes their activities and molds their lifestyle.

All worthwhile traditions need a patient dose of passing time. I'm a witness to the powerful effects of a long-standing family tradition, especially one that occurs outdoors. While traditions vary from area to area, they all carry the same purpose and are driven by the same desire.

The combination of family, nature, and tradition can leave a deep imprint within a person, regardless of your original location or final destination. It may seem hidden at times, but it's still inside you. It's your choice to bring it to life.

My reflections provide a deep appreciation for my life's path. However, my trout fishing trips remain prominent in my mind. Why is this? Perhaps it's because fishing a backwoods stream appeals to a person's spirituality in the most basic sense. There aren't any cell phones, video games, or mind-poisoning media. Information is gleaned by examining your surroundings instead of using Google. Decisions are based on common sense and experience versus pressing a button for direction. You depend on your instincts and teamwork with your partners to best a rugged wilderness. Clear air and clear thoughts rule the hours. I need this in my life. The next generation needs it even more.

Interestingly, during our annual family trips up North, we still continue our fishing ways. Among all our trips, one from six years ago stands out. Perhaps it was because I shared it with my younger brother and our sons, where a gorgeous day was amplified by non-stop brook trout action. Perhaps it was because the passing of our family's traditions took a foothold that day. Maybe it was special because our families and our parents greeted us at day's end; as it turned out, cancer claimed my mother's life the following year. That one excursion not only embodied a typical day on the stream, but it was a microcosm of our journey in life as we experienced triumphs, struggles, disappointment, mentoring, peace, and happiness.

That trip's significance may provide the answers I'm searching for. I want to continue contemplating, but I can only battle the Sandman for so long. Besides, sometimes puzzles are best constructed after a state of rest. With that, I finally plunge into an inviting nap, where warm memories can come alive.

2

Lightning Streaks

*A*n early morning August sun greeted my family and me as we left Proctor, Minnesota, and cruised down a long hill that overlooks the western tip of Lake Superior. Below us the towns of Duluth, Minnesota, and Superior, Wisconsin, rimmed the lake's tip and sprawled out before us; they lay dormant that early hour. From our vantage point, the sister cities were dwarfed by Lake Superior as it opened its arms and stretched forever, disappearing into the horizon.

My younger brother Jeff, nicknamed Nub, his son Drew, my son Alex, and I were poised for the day ahead. I appropriately labeled Nub with his lifelong nickname; it stemmed from an energetic little bear in the children's book *Nubber Bear*. It wasn't unusual to be Flag River bound with my brother, as he had been my main trout fishing partner since my college years. What made this trip more special was having our sons with us. They first tasted the Flag when they were eight, much like me. Now, after several years of trips, they needed smaller amounts of guidance and supervision, which was the natural progression that Nub and I had hoped for.

As we sped forward in Nub's '92 Ford truck, I stared off in the distance. Somewhere eastward along the south shore of the great lake, the Flag River flowed into the blue expanse. While the Flag's contribution to Lake Superior was but a relative trickle, its contribution to us was much more. Every summer we were drawn to the call of this river that was rich with family memories. It was a gift to have another day on the stream.

Visions of the Lower Flag's trout-laden waters bounced around in my head. Its slow, meandering current dissolved the worries from even the most stressed fisherman. I should know, for I had spent many a day there through my college years, either fishing it alone or with a partner. Family-named holes like the Hairpin Corner, The Logjam, and Ido's Stretch crossed my mind. I pictured my brothers as they yanked in rainbows around boulders at The Hairpin. I pictured my dad—Pops to us—as he climbed over fallen timber and searched for hidden pockets to fish at The Logjam. And then a scene with my grandfather emerged, as he stood stoically and pulled in a brown at Ido's Stretch, appropriately named after him. Now those were the days!

Other memories surfaced of more recent trips on the Upper Flag, where the river narrows and tumbles over a rockier path. It's where Nub and I took our sons on their first trip, introducing them to our craft. Under the river's grace, the brook trout acted with reckless abandon and we enjoyed the show as the youngsters landed one scrappy trout after another.

I had a treasure chest of good times, but it saddened me that our style of fishing was becoming a lost art. Few and far between were those who strapped on their hip boots and fought their way up a snarled river just to drift a worm for a twelve-inch inland stream trout. Trout fishing on a backwoods stream was tough work. On the surface, it didn't seem worth the effort, unless you were one of us.

We were worm fishermen. It wasn't glamorous. Our trips dirtied our hands and soiled our clothes, yet cleaned our minds. We fished in the summer months when the river was relatively low. Our style on the stream was paced, as it was nearly a sin to rush through a day of fishing.

Our close in, underhanded cast style contrasted with the figure of a fly fisherman waving overhead a long strand of line. Our technique used minimal casting space, which allowed us to thoroughly body check the Flag's brushy quarters. Unlike fly fishermen, bait selection was of minor concern for us, because for the most part, one worm was as good as another. Perhaps us worm fishermen are perceived as dull-minded for not varying our offerings, but then again, perhaps we are highly accomplished for having simplified the fishing equation.

We didn't sport fancy equipment, drive a showy powerboat, or compete in lake fishing tournaments for walleye or northern pike like some fishermen. There weren't any lodges, boat launches, groomed paths, or high-tech gadgets. We had something much deeper though, a family tradition.

With nearly sixty years' worth of trips under our family's collective belt, we still participated in this forgotten art with vigor. The brushstrokes of our family's craft were still enriching, making us whole, and healing the dull wounds inflicted by the modern world.

My thoughts faded as I gazed at the vibrating reflection of a Nut Goodie bar on the dash. That candy bar warmed our trips for years. It was Pops' favorite bar back when I was a kid, often sharing space on his dashboard as we bumped down a potholed Highway 13 towards the Flag. The confection was first brought to market in the early 1900s, coinciding with when Gramps entered the world.

In the back seat, the boys worked on their version of treats, as they snacked on Fun-Dips and slurped Dr. Peppers. Why they had to eat Fun-Dips so early in the morning was beyond me. Nub and I let this slight of character take place each trip because, well, they were kids, and because it was something they started some years back. So, we embraced it.

"Hey fellas, are the Fun-Dips helping your backs recover from the worm picking last night?" I joked.

"Mine's fine now," Alex replied as he stretched.

"How many dozen did we end up with?" I inquired.

"About ten," Drew answered.

I did some calculating. "We might need to buy more." I glanced at Nub. "It was good we each pitched in a bit."

"Yeah," Nub said, "we're bound by tradition I guess."

"We come from a long line of worm pickers alright!"

"That sounds really weird," the kids spoke up.

"Hey, Gramps and Pops picked worms for many years," I said. "Pops taught us the ropes early on. There's a bit of an art to it, wouldn't you say Nub?"

"You dang right. Most people don't have a clue."

Although we commonly used store-bought worms, we still clung to our long-standing ways of worm picking. We'd pick a night or two before our trip so the worms were fresh for their day of reckoning.

The key to a successful night out on the lawn was darkness and moisture. Our best nights were after thunderstorms, when the saturated ground forced worms from their holes. If we weren't blessed with rain, we'd water the lawn instead. On warm evenings, they'd be stretched on the grass, which made for easy picking. However, for the most part, worm picking was a challenge. Only a seasoned worm picker had a prayer at nabbing those lightning quick streaks. Even then, there were many times I missed and I was left holding blades of moist grass.

The serious pickers scooted around on their knees with a flashlight and an empty ice cream bucket. The "knee technique" provided a stable base for nabbing our prey. This technique led to wet pant legs, but it had a successful track record. We also experimented with the "standing" technique, but the worms were long gone before we bent down.

The earthworm is often called a dew worm or night crawler for obvious reasons. They have the girth of a drinking straw but are only half as long. Their downfall is that their slimy brown bodies glisten in the dimmest of light. A schooled veteran shines the beam at an angle and searches the shadowy edges for worms because they are sensitive to direct light. They often leave the scene as proof.

It's an art to steady the light and trap the worm with one hand. After a successful trap, the flashlight is dropped and the slippery creature is eased from its hole with two hands, and then plopped into a bucket. Sometimes a single-handed pull works, but the bugger often snaps. We don't keep broken worms because they usually die and spread disease.

We tried different containers over the years, but a plastic gallon ice cream bucket works the best. Coffee cans are serviceable, but they tip easily if bumped. Mom's Tupperware bowls worked too, but we'd have to sneak them from the kitchen. She had a royal fit when she found out. A desperate picker might stuff their pockets, but I draw the line there.

Worm picking typically kicks off our fishing trips. It's settle time, when we reminisce and talk about the next day, easing us into the trip's mental framework.

"Hey, did you ever pick worms with Gramps?" Nub asked.

"Man, you know, I don't remember for sure," I answered. "I tried in his back yard, but he wasn't with me."

"Did he have any hot spots like us?"

"Probably, but I couldn't point them out."

"Remember our go-to spots at Pops' house, like between the houses and under the lilac tree?" Nub asked with youthful enthusiasm.

"Oh yeah, those spots always came through!"

Nub sat deeper in his seat like he had just finished a big meal.

"I'm still thinking about Gramps' house," I said. "Remember that worm container he built against his basement?"

"That's right!" Nub exclaimed in a revved up voice.

Gramps had made an outdoor worm container that nestled against his house's foundation so he could pick at his leisure. He dug a hole against his basement window, lined it with a half circle of corrugated metal and filled it with dirt and peat moss to keep it moist.

Nub sported an inquisitive look. "Hey, didn't that basement have some kind of sausage hanging room?"

"Correct-o-mondo!" I turned to get the kids' attention. "Boys, here's a little piece of trivia for you. Your great grandparents had a special room in their basement where they hung their homemade salami and venison sausage for curing. A holdover from native Italy I'd guess. Pretty cool, huh?"

"Pretty weird," they quickly responded.

"Hold on fellas, that's not weird. That was your Italian

grandparent's way of life. Their parents did the same thing, and their parents before them," I reasoned.

"It's still weird," they repeated.

"Look, they lived more off the land than we do. Your great grandparents took pride in doing things for themselves instead of running to the supermarket. They drank homemade wine, made sausages, and had a good time."

Alex straightened up and spoke. "Well, nobody has a sausage room anymore. I've never heard of that. Plus, mom always goes shopping anyway."

I sensed an educational moment on the horizon. "OK. Fine. But what are we doing right now?"

"Ahh, we're going trout fishing. That's a no-brainer," the boys said as they waved their arms around in true Italian form.

"Ah-hah! Why are we going trout fishing when we could buy fish at the store?"

They paused and cobbled together an answer.

"We have fun and you guys have always gone. You know?"

"Oh, I see. So you two go trout fishing because it's fun, and because your family has been doing it for years," I said.

"Yeah, pretty much."

"Alright guys, maybe your grandparents had a sausage hanging room for the same reasons?"

Silence laced the back seat as their brain synapses popped.

I raised my eyebrows and cocked my chin. "Well?"

A mumbled "yeah" floated up to the front and sprinkled over us.

"Since you guys are young, you probably don't think about all this stuff. Just remember where you came from, and you'll be a better person for it."

I could tell Nub's inquiring mind was still at work.

"So, how much do you remember about that sausage hanging room?" Nub asked. "I was too young back then."

"Honestly, only a little. I walked into it a few times—no sausages though, dang it. It was small with a sandy floor and no windows. Pops remembers it well though."

Our grandparents designed their sausage hanging room when they built their house. The ceiling was six and a half feet high and irregular in shape because the room was built under the outdoor concrete steps that led into the house above. On each side of the steps was a baseball-sized hole with a mesh screen that allowed outside air to ventilate the sausage room below.

The grand event of sausage making took place in the fall, when the temperature was right for curing. Gramps had his own hand-turned meat grinder that mixed all the meats and spices. They made three-inch diameter salami sticks, tied the ends off with string, and hung them on nails that were in narrow wooden beams that ran across a five-foot wide ceiling. They also made venison sausage by stuffing meats and spices in a long, circular pig intestine casing. The circle ends were tied off and then the sausage was twisted about every four inches along its length to make links. The sausage circle was then hung on the nails to cure.

It took about two months to complete the curing process. Air humidity was key, which is where the sand came into play. Gramps checked the room often to ensure there was enough moisture to assist the curing process. If it became too dry he'd add water to the sand floor, which slowly evaporated, keeping a constant humidity level. Pretty clever I thought.

The sight of the finished product was a bit peculiar. In late fall, the sausage room showcased a bunch of moldy objects suspended from the ceiling at eye level. The mold was only on the outer skin of the sausage and was easily removed before eating. The aroma, however, was outstanding! The room's moisture accentuated all the smells that the herbs, spices, and meats could deliver.

Now that's Italian!

3

A Watchful Eye

*O*ur family history lesson halted as we pulled into the Bait Box in Superior, Wisconsin, for worms, licenses, and other stream fishing necessities. The stop was a mood setter before hitting the stream, as the familiar smells of a bait store seasoned our nostrils for the day ahead. Once inside, we shuffled through a small entranceway that led into a rectangular shaped building. The interior was wallpapered with fishing gear, and glass-door refrigerators boasted full racks of worms, salmon eggs, and other baits. Trout fishing-related jabber ricocheted off the walls, reinforcing our thoughts and soothing our minds as we sifted through the store. After some digging, we found what we needed and carried our load to the front, wrote up our licenses, and paid the bill to the ring of an old-fashioned cash register. An elderly gentleman, who moved at a trout fisherman's pace, closed the register's jaw and wished us good luck. Before we departed, I grabbed a Wisconsin Trout Fishing Regulations booklet to brush up on the rules.

As we drove, I thumbed through the booklet with controlled emotion, much like an older kid opening presents on Christmas morning. Wisconsin is home to a plethora of inland freshwater trout streams, however, not all streams have the same rules. It required some careful reading to stay legal.

I popped my head up and spoke. "Well guys, the rules for the Flag are like last year. Each person can keep five trout. Brookies have to be at least eight inches, browns at least ten, and rainbows twenty-six."

The kids were buried in their tasty Fun-Dips and barely heard me.

However, Nub perked up. "It's been that way for a while."

"Yeah. I'd say for at least twenty years. When I was younger, ten was the limit."

"I remember that alright," Nub added.

"Man, those were the days. Sometimes my creel got so heavy my back and shoulders hurt," I recalled.

He raised a finger. "And the rainbows. We kept the smaller ones back then."

"That's right. I think they had a ten-inch limit. Of course, that's back when they planted browns and rainbows. Now the brookies, they were always native."

"The rainbows and browns are slim pickings since they stopped planting," Nub pointed out.

"That's probably why the limit's been cut back. But we catch way more brookies now," I was quick to add. "They must do better naturally in the Flag."

"Remember when Gramps or Pops caught a brook trout? It was like finding a golden egg!"

I had to laugh. "Yeah, there weren't many brookies in the Lower Flag where they mainly fished, so when they got one it was a big deal."

"And those brookies have that reddish meat."

"Yeah, we all thought it was the neatest thing. They looked a lot different than the white meat in the planted trout."

My brother's face wrinkled. "That white meat was kind of soft. Sometimes it separated from the backbone when I cleaned those buggers. You had to be gentle with them."

"Maybe the fish pellets made their meat a bit mushy. That wasn't natural for them," I reasoned. "The brookie's meat is firm, and they taste better. Don't get me wrong, I enjoyed catching the planted fish, but natives are the best."

Lord knows how many times we had discussions of that manner. But they never got old. If anything, they grew on me like a comfortable beard. I hoped the kids paid attention while we chatted, so they could pass on stories to a fifth generation of Dincau trout fishermen.

The uptick in trout talk blended well with having left Superior, thereby swapping city sights for country sights. We turned east on to scenic Highway 13, which parallels Lake Superior's southern shore and leads to the Flag River. Groves of green-topped poplar, maples, and birch trees lined the paved road, occasionally giving way to a smattering of harvested hay fields. The roadside edge cradled rows of buttercups that popped with color; our passing breeze dizzied their arrangement. Fresh August air begged for attention, so I opened the window and let my fingers dance to the whims of the draft.

We were descending a broad hill when Nub pointed at a small stream that wormed out of the woods. "Hey, can you see that creek down there?"

I peered out my window, fighting the sun's glare. "Yeah, it looks pretty good. Low and clear."

We've seen Wisconsin's streams in other moods, angry moods, when a recent storm made a river claw at its red clay banks, turning a passive flow into a rust-colored torrent. A trout fisherman had no use for such stream conditions. We watched for those telltale signs as we drove.

"Did you look at the radar this morning?" I asked Nub while looking at my phone.

"Nah, I didn't have a chance, but last night The Weather Channel forecasted clear skies for Port Wing with a high of eighty degrees."

"Good deal." I still had a few bars of cell phone coverage, so I viewed the updated radar. "Clear as a bell," I said.

"Perfect. Hey, you remember back when we were teenagers? We stayed up for the ten o'clock news to catch the weatherman. Either that or we listened to the radio," Nub recalled.

"I sure do. Remember the bad toupee on that weather dude? That was hilarious."

"Sort of. What I really remember was he was wrong most of the time."

"Now look at us. I have real time weather in my hand. The heck with the toupee guy!" I exclaimed with a soft fist pump.

Nub verbalized more thoughts while he stared straight ahead. "You got to wonder."

"I wonder all the time. About what?"

"About technology. Where will we be ten or twenty years from now?"

I readjusted in my seat as the thought almost made me uncomfortable. "Who knows? Maybe they'll invent some wacked-out pair of glasses to see trout under the water."

"If so, I'm not wearing them!" Nub trumped.

"Neither am I. Some things just need to stay the same."

Our discussion was interrupted as the kids started up their own two-piece band behind us.

I turned to curb the commotion. "What the heck is going on back there?"

Alex fumbled with his soda and laughingly pointed at Drew. "Drew ate his Fun-Dip stick too fast. He tried to get the powder out with his fingers, and now it's all over his hands. Look at him! Ha, haa!"

A scowled expression draped across Drew's face. He was having none of that. "Yeah, well Alex spilled his pop and got his pants wet!"

I leaned back a bit more. "Look at you two. For crying out loud, you guys are the next generation of trout fishermen." I looked to Nub for some guidance. "Nubby, what gives here?"

He summed the situation up nicely. "You know what you guys are? Subordinates. Plain ole subordinates," he said while talking out the side of his mouth.

"Hey, that's a good one," I said with a grin. "We got a lot of work to do with those two. I didn't think we'd be passing the torch to a couple of pop-slurping subordinates."

We lightened up on the kids moments later. They knew we liked to joke around. There were some strong veins of humor that ran through our family, on both our parents' sides. One thing was certain, whether we caught our limit or not, we had fun. That was a chapter straight from the guidebook of Gramps and Pops.

After a flurry of more trout fishing banter, we fell silent as we drove down a steep, winding hill into a picturesque valley that owes its existence to the rapid flowing Brule River. For many fishermen and outdoorsmen, this is God's country. The Brule is a genetically gifted trout stream with over sixty miles of water. Cast with a dye of diluted root beer, its rock-filled bed is home to a healthy population of resident rainbow, brown, and brook trout along with seasonal lake-run browns and rainbows. The lower portion of the river, which is where we cross, offers wide stretches of open water and is often fly-fished from foot or canoe. The upper reaches of the river are spring fed and narrower, which would better lend itself to our worm drifting, but we had yet to explore that area.

I pointed towards the tumbling Brule as we drove over the Brule River Bridge. "One day we're going to fish that river. It looks so good."

Nub restrained himself from looking since he was driving. "It's funny, we say the same thing every trip, but we never stop."

"You're right. Gramps fished the Brule a few times, but he never talked much about it. It was probably too wide for him," I added.

"And it's big for steelhead fishing too. That wasn't Gramps' forte," Nub reminded me.

"Nah, he liked drifting worms in smaller streams in the summer. It was warmer weather and less people."

Steelhead fishing is a burning passion for many anglers in the northland. Every April, Lake Superior's rainbow trout are genetically drawn to their birth streams. They fight a torturous path up icy waters to reproduce. The annual spectacle draws hardy fishermen who hope for a fight with a lake-run brute. Steadfast figures lift their poles for one drift after another amid cold legs and stiff fingers. The weather might be nasty and the river sometimes crowded, but the hefty fish are considered a bragging-right icon.

We never got into steelhead fishing, and not because of the Viking-like elements. We braved worse times while duck hunting or deer hunting in northern Minnesota. No, the main reason we didn't tangle with steelhead was because it lacked family history. Pops and Gramps didn't enjoy it enough to pursue, and in the end, neither did we.

After another fifteen minutes down Highway 13, we were greeted by an expansive view of Lake Superior. Since Highway 13 parallels the lake's south shore, it offers scenic vistas of our country's largest body of freshwater. Lake Superior not only provides fine lake trout and salmon fishing, but it's also the final resting place for all streams that drain the northern Wisconsin highlands.

We approached a familiar wayside rest that was perched over the lake. It was a neatly groomed area with a few wooden picnic tables, a hand-operated water pump, and a restroom.

"Hey boys, there's the wayside rest with the great view. We'll stop there on our way back and have a snack. I ate there with your great grandpa on that same picnic table thirty-five years ago," I said while pointing left.

"Are we going to have our rock throwing contest too?" Alex asked.

I caught sight of him in the rearview mirror. "I suppose. You'd have to ask since you've won it the last four years," I replied with a sheepish smirk.

It's uncanny how a winner's memory is often razor sharp.

4

Mangiare!

*O*ur time on Highway 13 was nearing the end as we entered the small community of Port Wing. We cruised by the town hall, the Johnson Store, the South Shore High School and Elementary School, and a couple of eating and drinking establishments. The town hosts many other interesting places including two historic churches, a bed and breakfast, and a marina for easy access to Lake Superior. For a town of a few hundred people, Port Wing has a lot going for it. We've enjoyed its quiet and friendly confines for years.

Nubby slowed his truck to mimic the beat of the surroundings.

"It won't be long now," he said while rolling his hands over the steering wheel.

The Flag River crossed under the highway at the back end of town, but we wouldn't see it there because the Flagg River Road intersected the highway just beforehand. We pulled up and turned right on a faded maroon gravel road that led into the Flag River Valley. Roadside brush crowded our lane, while loose gravel went off like popping corn under rolling tires. As we motored along, I looked for some familiar landmarks that remained imbedded within me.

About a half-mile down the road was one of those places, in the form of an abandoned gravel pit. The floor was small as gravel pits go, but large enough to hold a few vehicles, a couple of tents, and a rip-roaring campfire. That unassuming sanctuary was a vibrant rendezvous place for our family back in my youth. I felt a strong desire to stop and soak up some memories.

"Hey Nubby, how about we pull over by the old gravel pit for a minute. I want to take a peek," I requested.

As he squinted and scanned to the right, the kids popped up to attention. A few moments later we slowed and parked at the edge of an overgrown flat area. The adjacent hillside's scalloped face was no longer dirt and gravel, but instead was bearded with trees and underbrush. To the casual observer, the area looked mundane. To me, it was much more.

My fondness for that spot was quickly tarnished, however. Smack in the middle of where we used to camp were two unsightly trespassers. I rolled down the window after the road dust settled.

"For crying out loud. Look at that!" I protested and pointed in disgust.

Drew pushed his head towards the front. "What are those things?"

Nub spoke in a sullen voice. "Looks like some kind of transport containers. Not sure how long they've been there."

Their elongated metal bodies stood side-by-side and pointed towards the road. Their squared ends were cold and steely eyed. Tall grass had grown around them as nature tried its best to conceal the intruders. It choked me up some.

"Fellas, this was my old camping spot with Gramps and Pops. We had some great times here—and now look," I groaned while my chin rested on my hand.

The gravel pit struck a chord with my brother also. "I missed those early camping trips, dang it. I was just too young." He looked back at the kids. "But we parked here on our day trips later on."

I perked up. "Yeah, we did. That's when the Lower Flag was hot."

"So you guys fished here all the time?" the kids asked.

"You bet. We usually started at the Hairpin Corner, which is just up a ways. One group fished downstream a half-mile to an old wooden snowmobile bridge. The other group fished upstream to The Logjam. Later, we'd all meet back at the vehicles."

Alex twisted his head back and forth. "Hey Dad, so where's the river from here?"

"It's just behind us, on the other side of the road."

"Yeah, it's maybe forty yards through the woods," Nub estimated.

"It's an easy walk," I said as I turned back and gazed at the gravel pit. "Yeah, we used this place a lot."

We sat a bit longer while the truck idled. Nub mumbled something and grabbed for the trout regulations booklet, while the boys seemed content as they joked around. That allowed me to reminisce about a time when I was the ripe old age of ten. A warm feeling flowed through my body as I recalled an overnight fishing trip with my father, Ray, my grandfather, Ido, and my grandfather's friend, Rizzy.

Etched in my memory bank was a campfire scene from back then. We sat around a fire pit littered with snapping embers, while in the background the static-laced drone of a Minnesota Twins game steadily pumped from Gramps' old radio.

The sun had neatly tucked itself behind the forest's canopy. Long shadows coalesced and transitioned into darkness, while a spray of stars sparkled against an obsidian sky. The night's cool air was a welcome guest after the midday heat, and fireflies innocently danced at the forest's edge.

The older guys' casual demeanor fit perfectly with their light flannel shirts and half-rolled sleeves. They leaned forward on their lawn chairs and passed stories back and forth with ease. A day of nice weather and great trout fishing added even more zest to their talk. I wasn't sure what it was about campfires and storytellers, but a jumping flame seemed to fan their tails. Vibrating waves of light dispersed from the campfire and illuminated their faces, making the adults look like a trio of happy-faced jack-o-lanterns.

"Hey Ray, did you and Rizzy fish beyond The Logjam?" Ido asked while he slapped a mosquito on his balding head.

Ray straightened up in his chair. A blue baseball cap wrestled with his dark mop of hair. "Nah, we had our limit by then. We caught some at The Logjam, and then I stepped in a deep hole and went over my doggone boot," he said while tugging the cap's bill. That move drew attention to his prominent Italian nose, which stood proud and silently boasted its heritage.

"Yeah, the evidence is over there," Rizzy laughed as he pointed to a saggy white sock that hung off the tailgate of Ray's '65 Chevy.

Moments later, the fire popped and a glowing piece of ash floated towards the sock as if it listened to the conversation. Its life came and went like a shooting star.

"We decided to hoof it back after that," Ray said. "Of course, Rizzy had to fish while we walked back. He never could count a limit of ten worth a crap."

Rizzy's short and stocky Italian body rose up in defense. "Hey, wait a minute. I can count just fine." The glowing firelight accentuated his flaming red hair. "I figured maybe Ido and Tony hadn't filled their creels, so I caught some insurance."

"Insurance my ass," Ray responded. "You just can't stop fishing and you know it."

"Aaww. You're full of it," Rizzy shot back as he waved Ray off.

They all sat back in their chairs and laughed.

I wasn't quite sure what to make of all the talk, so I sat still and kept a firm grip on a cold can of root beer.

"Well, what about you guys?" Ray asked Ido and me. "Did you get to the old snowmobile bridge?" he asked, while dancing flames reflected off his black-rimmed glasses.

Gramps gave me a glance and smiled while he answered. "Yeah, we made it. We had a great time. We needed a few more, so we fished beyond the bridge a ways."

"And we found a couple of nice holes that Gramps normally doesn't fish. We got our limit at those spots. Right, Gramps?" I asked and looked for approval with wide eyes.

"Oh, you dang right. You should have seen him catch those trout—just like we taught him. That's my boy!" he said, shaking his head and smiling in dramatic fashion.

I felt a bit embarrassed from the attention, but I felt proud too.

Gramps finished his Pepsi and stepped around the fire with his sights set on starting dinner. His figure hovered in the flickering dim light as he set up shop on an old fold-up table. He knocked the dust off his green Coleman gas stove and stoked it to an even flame. Near the stove were some leftover hard rolls, a few chunks of salami, a hunk of Asiago cheese, and two jars of homegrown pickled banana peppers—sure signs of Italian campers.

Rizzy noticed Ray's beer was empty so he took action. "Hey Ralphie, how about another piva?" Rizzy asked as he got up and swigged the remainder of his beer.

"Sure Riz. Sounds good."

He picked his way around the edge of camp and shuffled to the coolers. His profile was barely discernible in the softened darkness as he rattled among bottles and half-melted ice. He came back with two dripping cold beers and a bottle of brandy.

"How 'bout a horn, Ralphie?" Rizzy asked as he thrust the brandy in Ray's direction.

"Yeah, I'll take a snort," he eagerly responded with an outstretched hand.

Being an astute lad, I figured "piva" meant beer. I learned later that piva is a Serbian term, and that my grandfather and father grew up with Serbians back in their hometown of Gary-New Duluth. It turns out that "a horn" was a brandy or some other hard drink. A snort was their version of a swallow of brandy. I became schooled in Italian slang with a pinch of Serbian lingo and grew to love that talk. However, there was more to learn.

I left my chair and joined Gramps at the Coleman. "Hey Gramps, why did Rizzy call my dad Ralphie?" I whispered.

He looked down at me with raised eyebrows and a grin. "Aaww, that's just a fun and friendly name we call each other. No real reason for it. All of us good friends are Ralphies, I guess."

I gave Gramps a quick look and said, "Okay, Ralphie."

He got a "kick" from that reply and a hearty chuckle followed me back to my chair.

While the fire's heat lapped my pant legs, I tipped my head back and took a deep breath of fresh country air. My comfy state was short-lived, however.

"Hey Tones, are you ready to mangia?" Pops spoke up matter-of-factly.

Hmmm. Did Pops just ask me to dance?

"Ahh…well, are you ready to ahh, mangia, too, Dad?" I stumbled, hoping for another clue to his question.

"Yeah. Maybe you can get the insalata from the cooler and a big bowl." He pointed off in the night. "We'll get rolling on the fish and other things."

"Ray, did you pack the spuds?" Rizzy asked.

"Yeah, there's a bag in the back of my truck. I got a few cans of beans too."

We all left the campfire and went to work. I was certain insalata was salad, so I had that duty covered. But the mangia thing, well, it probably meant food or dinner or something like that. To clear that up, I slipped back over to Gramps and prepped the salad alongside the warming Coleman stove. We stood side by side under lantern light.

"Gramps," I said while looking up to him, "are you hungry?"

"Yeah, like a bear."

"So, you're like mangia hungry?" I asked in an uncertain tone.

He stood bolt straight in surprise. "Ho ho! Mangia you say? You betcha I'm ready to eat," he exclaimed while patting my back. He turned to Ray and Rizzy who mingled behind us and yelled, "Mangia, mangia!"

And they howled back in the night, "Mangiare! Mangiare!"

That's how our trips went. They were freewheeling, fun, and rather unique. Those gatherings had heart and soul that seeped deep within us.

As Pops often said, "You get an education out here that you can't get in the classroom." Well said, Pops, well said.

Later that evening, after a good dose of camp food and plenty of trout fishing talk, I drifted off to the shelter of Gramps' old canvas tent and befriended my soft sleeping bag. That special odor of old canvas lingered and reminded me that I wasn't bedded at home; it was another signpost of an outdoor adventure.

It wasn't often that I slept near the Flag River. The thought of its relaxed, steady current winding in the background put me out for the night.

My reminiscing at our old campground ended when Nub piped up, "Hey, you want to get moving?"

In an instant, the colorful characters that had filled my mind evaporated. All the laughter and camp equipment disappeared. The whiff of canvas had drifted off. The campfire was vanquished and the curtain of night was ripped open. In their places were weeds, bushes, and two metal beasts. A dull silence covered the area.

The stark contrast hit me. Why here and why now I wondered? Perhaps I fully sensed that nearly thirty-five years of time had swept through me. Is there anything more sobering than the full recognition of passed time?

My son and nephew now represented my youth, much like I had represented my father and grandfather's youth long ago. Only I had the experience to bridge my family's past in this area. It was important to continue our fishing trips and mold the next generation.

I leaned back and stared at the containers. Logically, I understood that all things eventually change, but it was still hard to swallow. I turned and watched remnants of our road cloud drifting off in the distance, its particles flickering amid a newborn sun—maybe we really are just dust in the wind.

5

The Trout Whisperer

*M*y brother slugged me softly in the arm. "Did you hear me? You want to get going?"

"Ahh, yeah. I suppose." I hesitated without expression, rolled up the window, and refocused on my crew. "Let's roll. We got some trout with our names on them!"

The boys were antsy as they wrestled with each other. It was definitely time to move on. Several blocks down the road a sharp left bend angled by a small pasture that used to be studded with crabapple trees. We slowed to negotiate the curve.

"Hey Nubby, do you remember the crabapple trees over there," I said while scanning to my right.

"Oh yeah. There used to be some big ones. That was a deer hangout too."

"No kidding. They love those things." I kept staring into the pasture. "There's still one barely visible. Grandma picked apples there for her apple pie you know."

"Really?"

"You betcha. Her apple pie was my all-time favorite," I said while licking my chops. "One slice of that baby could make a desert wind salivate."

"Alright, cut it out. I'm trying to drive here." He flashed a grin.

What was it about grandmas and their pies? They had that magic touch when it came to baking. And our grandma found her groove with apple pie. She had the perfect blend of sugar, cinnamon and spices. The crust was light and flaky, and those apples…mama mia, they were always soft and delectable.

"Turns out that Gramps took Grandma fishing once in a while," I went on.

Nub chuckled. "I know she didn't fish. What was her gig again?"

The thought of Grandma fishing was a bit silly. She cooked a mean pie, but she wasn't exactly fleet of foot.

"She stayed in the car and read. When she needed a break, she'd walk from the gravel pit where they parked and pick apples."

Alex leaned forward and spoke. "Why didn't she just drive to the apples?"

"Yeah," Drew said, "I mean, you said she was sitting in the car anyway."

Their hair was messed in a few spots from their tussle, but now they were attentive.

"Funny you should ask. Actually, even funnier that you were listening," I said with a satisfied expression. "Grams never learned to drive."

The boys slid their heads back in surprise.

"She stayed at home and didn't drive. I think they only had one vehicle and not much money. It worked for them. That wasn't uncommon back then."

"Wow, that's different," the boys exclaimed.

"Just remember, it's the times that were different, not so much the people," I said to them. "You may be more like your ancestors than you realize." More intensely, I noted, "It's good to know your past. Learn to appreciate it."

A half-mile later the Flag River crossed under a bridge and revealed itself to us. The river wasn't much wider than the bridge itself.

"Hey, let's pull over and take a look," I reminded Nub.

He didn't respond; he knew the plan. A heightened sense of concentration blanketed his face. We stopped on the bridge like clockwork on every trip. To mention it was just a formality. Nub guided us to the right rail and through open windows we all eagerly stared upstream. It was a flowing beauty.

"Well, what do you think, fellas?" I asked while watching the river.

Nub craned his neck and cast a searching eye. "The water looks good, real good," he emphasized while looking over a sandy-bottomed stretch.

Alex and Drew bobbed around like two quail and added, "Yeah, it looks nice and clear."

The Flag's version of clear wasn't exactly gin-clear, as it always carried a dusty olive hue, even during dry spells. Nonetheless, we considered the river to be in full form for worm drifting.

We navigated another bend in the road and passed a small rustic cabin, which marked "the road stretch". This short stretch paralleled the road and was easily accessible, which made it our favorite afternoon fishing spot. Nub slowed the truck to a crawl for us to view the water, which allowed me time to reminisce.

That stretch spurred thoughts of a heartwarming memory I shared with my grandfather, the original master of the stream. Approximately thirty-five years earlier I had watched in amazement as Gramps pulled six trout from one hole. They were piled up like cordwood under some logs, and I bore witness while he worked that trout lair like Picasso over a canvas.

As I fished from a sun-drenched sandbank, Gramps stood thirty feet upstream in knee-deep water, littered with blotches of shade. A slow-moving current pressed against his worn rubber hip boots and tested the seal of several homemade patches. He craftily positioned himself to drift his worm under some well-shaded logs and remain undetected by the fish. The olive-gray water gently boiled as it encountered the logs, casting a mesmerizing spell.

While he stood there in nature's gentle hand, it struck me that he literally became part of the river, as if he sprouted up and grew naturally like the vegetation around him. The river seemed to accept him as one of its own aged children. It was then that I hoped to grow up with this stream in the same manner that Gramps grew old with it.

I intently watched my sixty-four-year-old grandfather and studied his every move. His long-sleeved button-up shirt and dark slacks covered a slight frame, while an off-white fishing vest with bulging pockets hung casually over his torso. Hanging loyally by his left side was a wicker creel that occasionally flinched from a flopping trout. Around his waist, a brown leather belt fastened his green cylindrical worm can firmly to his front left hip. His balding head held a faded yellow ball cap that had a sewn-on patch in the front depicting a trout fisherman. His gold metal-rimmed bifocals were perched firmly on his nose, holding steady throughout all his movements. In his right hand he held his limber, seven-foot long black pole with grace, while his opposite hand gingerly stroked fishing line from the blue and gold Perrine automatic reel. On line's end were two split shot sinkers that sat above a piece of night crawler on a No. 8 single-barbed hook. The concentration on his tanned, whiskered faced was evident, much like an eagle eyeing his prey, yet there was still an easy way about him. He was a man in his element.

Gramps' motions were smooth and nimble. His first underhanded cast was effortless, almost timeless, as he pitched his line out like a fine silk thread. The arcing worm settled so lightly on the water's surface that it appeared to dissolve out of sight, seemingly beating the effects of gravity.

His first drift under a log sent his pole into convulsions as a thick, thirteen-inch brown trout slammed his bait. Gramps set the hook with a panther-quick wrist snap and deftly fought the fish to open water, keeping his rod tip up and his line taut. This technique helped keep the hook firmly planted in the trout's mouth. After a fiery tussle, the fish tired and Gramps gave him the "ole heave ho" to the brushy bank. Since he didn't carry a net, he typically banked the bigger fish. This, of course, sometimes led to nasty line entanglements, but it was worth it. Losing a nice trout was painful and frowned upon by Gramps.

Gramps laid the thirteen-incher in his new wicker home and went back for more. Not out of greed, but more out of duty. A few drifts later his pole tap-danced again as a scrappy twelve-inch brown fell victim to the master. Subsequent drifts led to several more smaller browns and rainbows that he released without leaving the stream. What a pro! He mastered the fine art of catching trout thanks to a combination of skill, experience, and a good dose of patience.

While Gramps worked his magic, my action slowed after I had caught a few.

"Pssst, Tony, sneak over here and try your luck," Gramps called and waved.

I stepped across the sandbank, skirted the brush edge, and slipped back into the stream beside him.

He pointed to where he'd fished and whispered, "Now it's your turn to read the stream."

I jokingly replied, "So, when does the next newspaper come floating by?"

It isn't that easy. Reading changes in water depth, current, and cover is an art that can't be mastered with books. Experience is the best teacher. Now successful veteran anglers, they learned to think like trout, like where they might hide and when they might strike. A trout's world is fairly simple—stay hidden, conserve energy, eat with care, and stay alive long enough to reproduce. An angler's savvy takes center stage when drifting a worm into a trout hole, not only by reading the water, but by feeling the line as it bumps off bottom and bangs into hidden cover. Since we can't see into most holes, with some being six feet deep or so, our sense of feel becomes our eyes under water, and that sense also triggers when to set the hook.

To watch a seasoned fisherman on his favorite stream, to watch Gramps at the Flag, was poetry in motion.

Inspired by Gramps' guidance, I flipped my worm into a shaded eddy that Gramps hadn't fished. The trout were getting the best of me when suddenly my pole bent sharply. Out of instinct, my wrists snapped upward for a clean hook set. The trout responded with rhythmic downward pulls that eventually eased as the fish tired. Moments later I gave a flipping, ten-inch brown a heave-ho to the nearest bank and then pounced on it immediately.

Gramps yelled to me, "Hey-hey Tony, Feesh-On-Ralphie!" That

excited stream call was our family patent that we used whenever we hooked a defining fish. The term Feesh, of course stood for fish, but in true "Ralphie" style, Gramps added a little flair to his stream lingo.

While I quivered from my catch, Gramps moved closer and slapped a tanned hand on my shoulder and exclaimed, "That's my boy, that's my boy!"

Later on, as we cleaned our fish on the river, Gramps gave me a silver pocketknife. That small knife came from the Wabegon Bar and Grill where Gramps worked and it represented a merit badge on the stream. Now that's how to hook a kid on fishing!

I had a number of landmark trips with Gramps; often it was just the two of us buried deep in the woods. Most of our trips were to the Flag, but occasionally we fished the Blackhoof River and Silver Creek down Highway 23 in Minnesota, just south of Gary-New Duluth.

I learned to appreciate Mondays because that was Gramps' day off work. I spent many summer Mondays with Gramps on the stream when I was between eight and fourteen years old, with Grandma always greeting us at trip's end. That's an important timeframe for a youngster, as my mind was being molded and my world's view was being shaped. Fortunately, I had a set of grandparents that complimented my parents, and they left a wholesome mark on me. The timing and effectiveness of my mentors' tutoring along with my natural attraction to the outdoors "locked" me into the Flag for life.

The timing of when Gramps became locked into the Flag isn't so clear. His fishing adventures began in the mid '50s when he was nearly forty-five years old. He didn't have the luxury of being introduced to the stream by his father, who had passed away from pneumonia when Gramps was in ninth grade. Being the oldest of five kids, Gramps was forced to leave school and work to financially support his family.

Gramps became very active with the outdoors after he was married. He enjoyed trout fishing in the summer, but also pursued rabbit and grouse hunting in the fall and winter. However, most trips were with friends. He was a fun-loving guy and he developed a close bond with his buddies over the years, partly because of his personality, and partly because he lacked a father to bond with.

Fortunately, Gramps and his buddies discovered the Flag and built a rapport with the stream with each passing summer. After Gramps became Flag savvy, he introduced his sons, Pops and Rocky, to the stream. Their younger sister Bonnie never did fish the Flag, but she found favor with the trout at the dinner table.

While Gramps and his sons had varied outdoor interests, none matched the blossoming tradition at the Flag. It touched four generations. Over time, single day trips turned into overnight camping trips, with each outing becoming a calendar event. Adventurous stories stacked up and grew a life of their own. Gramps didn't realize that those early days on the Flag would lead to many more years of fishing, connecting us all as one.

6

Baaal-loouu Sky!

*N*ub stepped on the gas and we left the road stretch behind. We negotiated some uphill curves and cruised along the upper portion of the Flag River Valley, which nestles against the beautiful Chequamegon National Forest and its mix of towering hardwoods and pines.

Shortly afterwards, we descended back into the valley at a slow pace, and for good reason, as nature sent us some pint-sized treats. A mother ruffed grouse and her brood stood at road's edge and scampered back into the woods as we drove by. The ruffed grouse, which is the size of a chicken, is a popular game bird in the area. Those munchkins added a perfect touch to our storybook scene.

Nub waved outward and asked, "Just think, we have the whole area to ourselves. I mean, how many times have we run across another fisherman on our trips?"

"Just a handful," I answered.

The truck nosed its way along a narrowing gravel road and came to a halt within a stone's throw of the stream. We parked in seclusion, while the spindly road continued by bridge over the river and ran for miles, much to the delight of ATV riders.

Under a patchwork of shade, we piled out of the truck and were greeted with wild beauty. Sentinels of aspen, poplars, and birch rose above the heavy underbrush and stretched towards a brilliant blue backdrop. In the background, the light roar of rushing water echoed off the Flag River's banks.

While we milled around and stretched our legs, a sharp noise pierced the air.

Doink! "Yeah, right in the middle!" Drew shouted.

"That was all luck," Alex replied as he threw a rock at a dented old road sign.

"Ha! You missed!" Drew heckled.

Alex threw a few more. Doink. Doink. "Yeah! Two in a row!"

"Hey fellas," I called. "Let's unload the gear and get going."

They responded, but only after they emptied their hands of ammo.

"Like herding cats sometimes with those two," I said to Nub while he dropped the tailgate.

"That's kids for you," Nub reasoned. "It's not like we haven't hit that sign ourselves."

"Yeah, I guess we started it."

The sight of four energetic fishermen grabbing trout fishing gear from the truck bed was nothing short of organized chaos. The cargo was a smorgasbord of rubber hip boots, poles, creels, containers of worms and a few coolers, among other items.

"Hey Drew, how about you hop in the truck and pull the cooler closer to us before putting your boots on." Nub said as he pointed.

"Aaww," Drew complained as he laid his boot back on the ground.

"Come on, it's easier for you young guys to do that stuff," Nub lightly snapped. "And don't step on those poles in there."

"Alex, why don't you help him out?" I suggested while I looked for my gear.

After Alex cleared a path, Drew moved the cooler to the edge of the tailgate.

"You want the worm bucket?" Drew asked as he jumped off the truck.

"Yeah," Nub responded. "And make sure you boys pack a water bottle with your lunch. We'll be back there for hours."

"Alex, can you reach that creel and vest for me?" I asked. "You know, those are your great grandpa's originals, including the green worm can inside the creel."

"Yeah, I know. I think you told me that a bazillion times before," he said with a soft grin.

"Oh, okay. Well, in case I forgot to tell you, this pole and reel I'm holding were his too," I said ribbing him.

The gear discussion piqued Nub's attention. "It's amazing how well some of this old equipment has held up. We've made a few minor repairs over the years, but nothing some duct tape, wire, and leather straps couldn't fix," he proudly proclaimed.

Our family's original equipment is sacred with us, being imprinted with layers of our fingerprints. Using the time-tested equipment bonds us to our forefathers and their early ways. We occasionally use new gear, but only when necessary.

Alex handed me Gramps' old wicker creel.

"Just look at this baby, guys. They don't make creels like this anymore!" I bragged while hoisting it high.

I gazed at the sturdy basket as if it were one of my own children. After all, that creel had ridden the side of my grandfather, father, and me for over fifty years. Perhaps my son would be the next to tote that relic up the stream.

Its heavy wicker weave carried a tone of worn straw. Ink black streaks filled the crevasses of the wicker fabric from having swallowed the sweat and soil left upon it by its masters. Its design was intelligent, as it was wider at the base than the top. This allowed more space to store fish and made it difficult for them to escape. The back was flat so it rode comfortably along the wearer's side.

The cover flipped open with ease and was secured by a small, sturdy buckle in the front. It had a convenient rectangular hole to drop fish through. The outside portion of the cover was lined with dark leather, and a wide leather band ran down the middle of the basket, which secured the buckle and connecting strap. The basket beamed with rugged, stylish beauty.

A long, looped leather strap connected through the basket's back so it could be hung over a shoulder. That piece eventually wore out and was replaced, however, the resting pad portion was salvaged. The dark leather pad was a generous three inches wide and its inside was lined with white lamb's wool for cushion. Over time, the wool lost some of its whiteness and the compacted fibers lost some of their fluff, but it was still the best shoulder companion around.

Nub leaned into the truck bed and pulled up another creel. "Yeah, the newer versions look more like this."

I shook my head. "Our old creel is a beast compared to that one."

"And it's bigger," the boys chimed in.

Nub rubbed his hand along the new basket's covered edge with a craftsman's care. "Cheap leather lining," he blurted out. "Actually, it looks synthetic. Heck, even the buckle is flimsy. Its days are numbered out here."

I stepped back for a moment and gazed at the sky.

"Hey guys, look up there."

"Up where. At what?" the kids asked as they looked about.

"Up at the sky. Look how blue." I glanced back at my brother. "Nubby, you remember what Gramps and Pops used to say on a day like this?"

He took a deep breath and blurted out, "It's a baaal-loouu sky!"

"That's it. It's a baaal-loouu sky for sure. Ha-haa!" I said.

The kids stared at us.

"Why did they talk like that? Balue sky," they repeated and fumbled the phrase.

I stepped closer to the boys and corrected them. "It's baaal-loouu sky. That was their stream lingo. It was their style; it made the trips even more fun." I paused with some reflection. "Actually, they said that kind of stuff whenever they were hunting or fishing. I mainly heard it out here though."

While we finished donning our gear, I reminded the boys of a trick that Gramps taught us when putting his two-piece fishing rod together. We fished with seven- to eight-foot long two-piece poles, but sometimes the rod wouldn't separate at day's end. So, before Gramps began fishing, he rubbed some natural oil off his nose and applied it to the top half end of his fishing pole. The thin film of oil acted as a natural lubricant between the adjoining pieces and allowed for easy separation. The simplicity and ingenuity of that maneuver stood the test of time.

As a pack of pesky mosquitoes got the best of the kids before we entered the woods, Alex asked, "Dad, where's the bug dope? These things are starting to bite."

"Check your vest pockets, and give yourselves a good dose. I've had a few trips totally ruined because I either ran out of bug dope or I forgot it," I told everyone. "Spray your face too."

"That's gross," the kids uttered.

"Just close your eyes, roll your lips inward, and blow out your nostrils while you spray and you'll be fine," I instructed.

They each fumbled around in their vest pockets looking for their bug potion. They got the message.

7

Three's Company

*W*e slipped through a narrow opening in the woods, holding our poles forward so they were easier to guide through the brush. Thankfully, we all were fairly lean and athletic because navigating through the woods with trout fishing gear and a lunch was not for the faint of heart.

I wasn't sure if we walked to the stream, or if it drew us to it. Perhaps it was a combination of both, like two old friends overdue for a visit. This trout stream was a personal place that appealed to the spirit, and the initial hike was not to be rushed, but rather savored instead. We never invited a stranger to this stream, just as we never invited a stranger into our homes.

After picking our way through the underbrush, we stood over the East Fork of the Flag River. This fork, which we commonly called the left fork, was slightly smaller than the right fork. The split in the forks occurred several hundred yards downstream from our location and was marked by a gorgeous, swirling hole that we occasionally fished.

We considered the "Forks" the upper portion of the Flag River. These stretches of stream had some notable differences from the lower portion of the Flag. The Upper Flag had pockets of faster flowing water and was narrower and rockier than the Lower Flag. The Upper Flag also contained mainly brook trout, while brown and rainbow trout ruled the Lower Flag.

The Lower Flag was our "bread and butter" back in the 1970s

and '80s. Those years were so productive that Gramps and Pops rarely fished above the swirling hole at the Forks, staying mainly downstream on the Lower Flag. That's where my trout fishing career began. Unfortunately, that all changed when the Wisconsin DNR cleared most of the logjams to reduce springtime flooding problems, thereby removing many of the trout holes. Around that same time, they ceased planting rainbows and browns that populated the Lower Flag. We adapted to the changed stream conditions and now mainly fish the Upper Flag, which has been a windfall for brookies. My son and nephew, due to timing and circumstance, cut their teeth on the Upper Flag.

We opted to fish downstream from the bridge to work out the kinks before heading back upstream into the thick of brook trout country. After testing several holes with minor success, the four of us walked back to the bridge and reconvened. The antsy boys couldn't wait to head upstream to where a deep, bending stretch of water offered ample trout holes. Before we parted, Nub reminded them of another old trick.

"To help keep your fish fresh, stuff your creels with some of those waist-high green ferns in the woods. Then dunk your creel once in a while," he encouraged.

I patted them on the back. "Good luck boys. When you two finish a hole, just walk upstream past us and fish the next hole you find. We'll do the same. Just take your time."

"Those boys are two peas in a pod," I stated as the blue jean-clad duo wandered off and disappeared in the brush.

"You're right. They're both so easy going and they get along great. And Alex is what, fourteen?"

"Yeah, and with Drew being big for his age, you wouldn't know he's three years younger. It's really cool they both like to fish and hunt." I tapped his shoulder. "I guess the apples didn't fall far from the tree, huh?"

"Yeah, there's something to that alright," Nub replied with a nod.

Before surrendering to the stream's call, we discussed fishing with four of us on the same fork. Normally, we fished both forks simultaneously in father-son pairs, but today we wanted to share our time together and give the maturing boys more freedom because they'd be on their own in future trips.

We decided to move at a slower than normal pace, which would afford the boys maximum fishing time. Our cups would be better filled knowing this. Our forefathers handled us brothers in the same fashion.

With that thought, my youngest brother Mitch came to mind. Unfortunately, he couldn't make the trip. He lived four hours south of the stream in the suburbs of Minneapolis. That's a long haul to chase stream trout. While Nub and I fished often over the years, Mitch only accompanied us a few times. Nonetheless, he dropped plenty of trout into his creel on other trips.

As a young adult, Mitch fished southern Minnesota streams and took a number of ten-day trips to Colorado, Wyoming, and Montana with a few friends. They fished some big streams like the Yellowstone and taught themselves the art of dry fly fishing. They drowned a worm or two also.

Mitch left Proctor to work in Minneapolis at eighteen years old, which limited his ability to fish the Flag. Since Gramps passed away when Mitch was seven and Pops was busy raising a family, Mitch missed some memorable trips and never got "locked in" to the Flag. He was hardly old enough to remember the few family trips he did experience. He dabbled with some trips in his early teens, but it didn't stick.

He was dealt a different set of cards than me through timing and circumstance. Perhaps our roles on the Flag were merely decided by birth order. I can only wonder. In a large way, we are what we experience, and our lives are shaped by situations born from uncontrollable factors.

"You know, it's too bad Mitch isn't here with us, eh Nub."

He shuffled his feet at the thought. "Yeah, it's hard for him to get up here for a day trip. It's kind of funny, but he's the only one that got into fly fishing. I know he caught some nice trout outside the Twin Cities area."

"If I remember right, Mitch caught some browns that were measured in pounds versus inches. And he used some top end gear, not like us backwoods stump busters," I said in a lighter tone.

"Yeah he did. It would be tough fishing dry flies out here though—a lot of brush and tight quarters," Nub pointed out.

"Yeah, none of us ever took to a fly out here. Heck, Mitch stayed with the worm when he fished with us."

We carried some respect for the often trampled on, lowly worm, for we'd be light in the creel without them.

Our few trips with Mitch were memorable. My youngest brother was a suave fisherman, sporting high-end sunglasses and a stylish ball cap. He proudly donned one of our older vests and worm cans, however, because he respected our ways like the rest of us. Being a trendsetter, on one trip he went shirtless, wearing only a vest. He sported a rough, Gucci-Tarzan look that was a fashion first for the stream. A hooked trout brought about a quick smile as he fired off his version of "Feesh-On-Ralphie" that rattled our ears and warmed our backwoods adventure.

Even though Mitch had limited exposure to the Flag, he read the water and fished the holes in a veteran's manner. I didn't quite understand it; maybe it just ran in our blood. He fed off the mud, sweat and scratches like his elder brothers, which added a sense of belonging to all of us.

We measured the value of our trips not so much by fish count, but by time spent together in our family refuge. It resembled a retreat of sorts, where we left the measures of everyday life behind. The river accepted us as we were, with all our imperfections, with all our differences. It just didn't matter out there.

As in many families, my brothers and I were hardly carbon copies of each other, and yet we had an underlying likeness that kept us bonded. I was the eldest with a four-and-a-half- year head start on Nub and a seven-year lead on Mitch. We shared likeness through athletics, the outdoors and sense of family. We were a passionate group that enjoyed good times with friends and family alike. A good dose of humor was common among us. As brothers go, we were a fairly close-knit set of kin.

In our school-aged years, our athletic prowess often put us boys in the same room, much to the chagrin of our dear mother. We turned our two-story home into a multi-level playing field. The basement held many floor hockey games and some wrestling matches. Our small kitchen was just big enough for some hand hockey games with a cushy ball. We used the harder ball when Mom wasn't looking. The dining room was host to Nerf basketball games and more wrestling matches. Our living room was a mainstay for tackle football, and sometimes we pulled Pops into the action. Mom basically left the house at that point to "go for a walk." Our greatest WWF wrestling matches occurred in the living room also. One time we ripped Pops' t-shirt off his back and into shreds. The joy! We used our staircase as a sliding hill, now that was noisy but great fun. The stairs led up to another hallway, where we played more hand hockey after we were booted from the kitchen. Our bedrooms were too small to do anything but sleep, and of course bounce off the beds and…wrestle. By the time we were adults we knew each other quite well.

Of course, we had our spats like all brothers in a household. In my opinion, when we weren't having fun, they were annoying little troublemakers. A cracked knuckle on my right hand was proof. After all, when Nub sat on my face and smashed my glasses in laughter, I had to react. Correct? It turned out his head was harder than my roundhouse right, and as the "law of older siblings" worked, I still got in trouble. Mitch was too young to mess with, so Nub handled that duty, but maybe a bit too often. I didn't think Nub's pummeling of Mitch was always necessary, especially in public settings—like church. On the rare occasion my younger brothers ganged up on me, I taught them both a lesson. I was satisfied until the law of older siblings kicked into gear and my parents lambasted me again. Oh well.

Undoubtedly, our Flag River fishing trips provided a good outlet for us boys to interact in a rugged and playful manner, much like during our youth. We didn't use a football or puck, but instead a fishing pole and creel. We stopped wrestling with each other, and instead wrestled with nature's tangled confines. In both cases, we ended up exhausted but smiling. Perhaps our fishing trips had deeper ties than I realized.

8

Feesh-On-Ralphie!

I concluded my brotherly thoughts with warm recollections. We began picking our way down to the stream when both of us went sliding down the seven-foot embankment with the grace of two blindfolded ostriches. We felt somewhat embarrassed after that debacle, especially after we had pounded into our boys' heads how important it was to be stealthy while navigating the stream.

Once on solid footing in the stream, Nub spoke up with disappointment. "Well, that slick move wasn't part of our plan."

"You're right there. We don't need a repeat performance later today either."

Trout are a wary species, and are easily spooked. That aggravates the galoot of a fisherman, but delights a light-stepping veteran motivated by the challenge. Because the Flag's banks are so choked with brush, we often stayed in the stream and slowly walked to the next hole. Our stream walking muddied the water, which was carried downstream. Therefore, we typically fished upstream to keep the water ahead of us clean, which helped prevent spooking the trout.

The spring-fed river welcomed us with a cool grip that wrapped around our legs. We breathed in the earthy, water-cooled air and let the sounds orchestrated by the stream settle our minds.

While nature's gentle music crooned, we scanned upstream, or read the water as we were taught. Up ahead, a few knee-high boulders peaked out from the river's surface and spun eddies off their moss-covered sides. The massive pieces of rock had originated somewhere in Canada and were left behind from the last glacier ten thousand years ago. Masses of green foliage intruded over the stream's edge, while a morning mist eerily hovered over the stream's shady parts. That combination challenged our professional water reading skills.

"You see anything to fish?" I asked Nub.

"It's hard to tell, but there might be a spot in the fast water ahead," he answered, straining his eyes.

"Yep, I see what you mean."

In a shaded bend, the olive-gray stream raced around a sandy point bar and dug into the opposite bank. It was a few paces short of twenty feet wide at that point.

"Hey, let's take the slow pony up there and give it a try," Nub said.

"Sounds good."

I took the lead and stumbled on a loose rock right out of the gate. "Watch out for the rocks," I warned.

"Gotcha. And keep an eye out for those clay patches too."

We used our feet to feel for unstable rocks, or worse yet, for patches of hardened Lake Superior red clay, which is another present left behind from the last glacial event. The red clay is widespread across northern Wisconsin and northeastern Minnesota, blanketing the region's bedrock.

It is typically very sticky, however, sometimes the clay platelets adhere together, making the clay mass hard and very slippery. We didn't want any part of those hazardous patches.

We walked a dozen more steps when Nub had another reminder. "How about those soft spots too?" We both stiffened at the thought.

"Oh yeah, I've gone over my boot stepping in those things."

"Me too. It's a weird feeling isn't it?"

"Yeah, like being in quicksand."

Unfortunately, all Dincau fishermen have stepped in soft spots and had their breath taken away. Since the Flag is spring fed, those areas are likely seep points of natural springs where continuously upward moving water keeps the sediments from compacting. They are typically the size of a large serving plate. We always escaped the hazards, but some incidents were more eventful than others.

"Hey, did you remind the boys about the soft spots?" I asked Nub.

"Nah, I didn't think of it—they'll be alright."

We worked our way to the point bar, keeping a low profile as we studied the rapids and undercut bank.

"What do you think?" I asked.

"How about I start up top?" he asked, gesturing to the beginning of the rapids.

After my thumbs up we took our places.

He pulled some extra line from the reel, made a well-placed underhanded pitch ahead of the rapids, and let his worm bump its way downstream. His right hand firmly gripped the pole while his left hand softly held the line outside the reel. In that manner, he could feel the slightest nibble and yet still set the hook in a moment's notice. We were taught that technique and it became second nature to us as we grew older.

I fished the lower part of the hole where the rapids dissipated. My automatic reel croaked as I yanked line from the spool. I laid an easy pitch towards the far bank and worked the bait back at a snail's pace. While doing so, my pinky finger touched the reel's metal lever underneath the body and automatically pulled in the slack line. It was a simple but efficient set of motions that we repeated often. A few light nibbles visited my line, but nothing too exciting.

After a few unsuccessful drifts, Nub's body twitched as he set the hook on a nice trout.

"Feesh-On-Ralphie!" he roared.

The trout tried to stay in the rapids and use the water's force to help its cause, but the fisherman outmuscled him. He leaned back and kept his line taut as he brought in the fish. His gear rattled and water droplets flew through the air while he ushered the trout to dry ground.

"Wow. That's a beauty!" I said.

He wrestled with the spunky trout in his hands. Once he had a firm grip, he unhooked it and dug around for his tape measure.

"Don't lose that thing," I warned.

"It's a twelve-incher!"

"A brookie?" I asked while I kept my rod tip in sight.
"Yeah. Take a look."

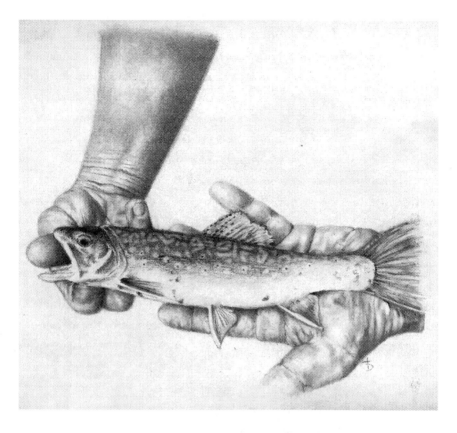

Nub's Prize—by Amanda Dincau

He crunched over to me with his catch, his pole pinned tightly to his side. I stepped back towards him as he held out the brook trout with both hands like the proud father of a newborn. A slight tremor rippled through his hands as he fought back an adrenaline rush from the fight.

I locked my eyes on the trout. "Look at the markings on that one. That'll keep for sure!"

The fish remained still as if it enjoyed the attention, but it was time for Mother Flag and her offspring to say goodbye, so Nub slipped the trout into his wicker basket. The trout responded with a few good tail slaps against the creel's stiff walls.

"Man that was a nice one," I said. "What a way to start the day, huh?"

"Yeah, if we keep this up we'll have a heck of a trip."

I wished we had brookies down South. While Cajun Country was blessed in many ways, it wasn't blessed with brook trout. And with the lack of cold freshwater down there, things weren't changing anytime soon.

We both turned away and I resumed drifting the slow current before me. In no time, I felt the tick-tick-tick of a smaller trout nibbling. I snapped my wrists after a heavier pull and hooked a lively eight-incher that put up a good little fight.

"Ho-hoo, Nubby, Feesh-On-Ralphie!" I echoed back, holding tight to my bent pole.

The trout emerged from the drink and danced over the water, spraying droplets across the river's face. Stream trout were scrappy, but with a firm hand, they could be landed fairly quickly.

"Here's another beauty," I said while holding it towards Nub. "Just look at the color on this one. I wonder why some trout have deeper color and better markings than others?" I angled the fish so the sun's rays enhanced the hues.

Nub looked my way as I released it. "Yeah, I've noticed that over the years. I'm not sure why, maybe its genetics."

They were truly beautiful creations, and I always gawked at my initial catch before releasing it back into its current-riddled dwelling. Its greenish-brown back and sides gave way to a white belly with tinges of yellow. On its back was a distinctive vermiculated pattern, which resembled random squiggles of a doodling artist. The flanks of the fish contained numerous yellow dots that were mixed with a sprinkling of red dots. The red dots were unique because they were surrounded by light blue halos. The lower fins carried a striking dark amber hue that finished in a line of black, only to be tipped in bright white at the bottom end of each fin. A square-like tail gave the animal a stylish, yet powerful look.

While some trout end up in our fry pans, we often practice fish conservation with catch and release. If they swallow the hook, we cut the line to enhance their chance of survival.

As Nub worked the rapids at different angles, I stepped up my game by sliding a cast near the root-infested bank so I could "feel" my way into the "danger zone", where many an angler's hook had fallen victim to the teeth of snag central. After several fruitless attempts, I worked up enough courage to test the deepest confines of the undercut. My eyes widened as midway through the drift I felt a bump and reacted with a quick, wrist-snapping motion to set the hook. My brief adrenaline pump turned into disappointment. A wily trout apparently nipped at the worm and fled the scene before the hook set, which resulted in a nasty, root-entangled snag. A few yanks on the line got me nowhere.

I gave an agitated glance towards my partner. "Dang it, I'm hung up. Are you finished working the rapids?"

"Yeah, I guess so. I've only had a few small bumps since I caught the first brookie."

"Okay. I'm moving into the hole to free my hook."

I inched closer to the snag until the river flirted with the top of my hip boots, and jabbed my pole in the water, hoping the rod tip would push past the entrenched hook and pop it free. This technique led to a broken rod tip once years ago, but it has also freed me from many snags. It was worth the risk. After several stabs, line pulls, and rod jiggles, I was still hung up. I was forced to break the line, and thereby declare Mr. Stream Trout the victor this time.

I retreated to the sandbar, tied on a new hook, and attached two new silver lead sinkers. The retie process is aggravating. It's tedious work that requires a steady hand and concentration. I stood still and pinned the pole against my body while unzipping the vest pockets that held the hooks and sinkers. The reel stayed suspended because a drop in the sand or a dunk in the river could turn a smooth operating automatic reel into a mechanical nightmare.

Small hooks, small sinkers, small pockets and big fingers lead to a red-faced fisherman on occasion, but a seasoned veteran finishes in a matter of minutes. That is, if the "mosquito siren" doesn't go off. This phenomenon has plagued the Dincau fisherman for generations. For some reason, a snapped line acts as a dinner bell for the feisty creatures. Perhaps they sense a defenseless fisherman. Countless times I fumbled with my gear while a swarm of mosquitoes materialized from thin air and proceeded to drill holes in my head, neck and hands. I'd shake my head, blow on my hands, rub my cheeks on my shoulder, and blow more air up the front of my face. I looked ridiculous.

Nub had moved above the rapids and hooked a trout while I was mired in fishing tackle and a dangling line.

"Feesh-On-Ralphie!" he fired off.

I lifted my head just enough to see his pole dancing. "Yeah, yeah, I'll give you a Feesh-On-Ralphie, alright," I muttered under my breath.

I didn't mind my partner catching fish, as long as we fished together. It was pure torture to watch and not partake. After what seemed to be an eternity, I was fit to fish again. I slogged thirty feet upstream to Nub.

"What did you catch here? You didn't say much," I asked.

"Just a small brown. I tossed it back," he said matter-of-factly.

"Oh. So, you ready to head out and catch up with the boys?"

"Yeah, this is a one-trout hole. Let's hit the woods."

We fished that stretch for ten minutes or so, which was about average for any given hole.

Off we went in search of the next adventure.

9

Top Banana

We headed upstream looking for the easiest route into the woods. A narrow break in the brush afforded us the opportunity. The best off ramps included some roots for a foothold and some hanging branches for a handhold. Both were available at that break, and we shimmied our way up the clay slope and stood at the bank's edge. However, I stood a bit crooked because of a hunk of red clay that clung to my boot bottom.

I slapped Nub on the arm. "Look at this stuff. It's sticky as heck. It's just a pain."

A well-placed deadfall with corrugated bark made for a good boot cleaner. After a quick boot scrub, we skirted through a knotted forest, stepping over deadfalls and brushing off unwelcome handshakes from some spruce trees. Toting trout gear and seven- to eight-foot poles made plowing through the woods even tougher.

We stopped for a breather. "You know, this forest gets thicker every year," Nub said.

"Well, maybe it just feels like it. We aren't getting any younger you know."

We resumed our pace and peeked over the stream to locate the boys.

"I don't see them," I exclaimed, "but they're near. There are two sets of fresh boot prints on the sandbar. And check out all the deer tracks."

"Yeah, a favorite drinking spot."

We went down for a closer look at the pockmarked sand.

"Nubby, do you see any boot marks older than the boy's prints?"

He snooped around like Sherlock Holmes. "Not really. I don't see any raindrop impressions anywhere either. It's been pretty dry."

"That's the way we like it." I pointed towards the river. "Hey, take a look at those terraces at the sandbar edge. Those things form when the water drops, you know. I betcha it hasn't rained in a while."

Nub straightened up and concluded, "The trout should be starving today. It's probably been at least a week since they've had a good feed."

A heavy rain always knocks bugs, worms, insects and other food into the stream, which often ignites a trout feeding frenzy. A good crack of thunder rings the trout's dinner bell.

Some of our most productive trips are during dry spells or just before pending thunderstorms.

"Come to think of it, the trout hit hard in that last hole and their bellies were flat. Their stomachs are probably empty," Nub reasoned.

"Speaking of catching trout, let's try this big hole the boys just fished," I suggested. "I'd like to see how well they fished this deep bend."

"Sounds good. We've always gotten something out of here."

That hole barely breathed a current and was lit with an olive-green hue. The deeper, darker water covered an unusually large area and was choked with an array of logs, branches, and roots. It was a tranquil picture that held some underlying secrets.

We crept to the water's edge, yanked line from our automatic reels, and pitched our baits towards the far bank. The weak current couldn't push the worms downstream, so they sat undisturbed, but not for long.

My pole bent sharply and then relaxed. "Wow, I just felt something heavy!" I said.

Nub took a step back. "Like what? A snag, a fish, or what?"

"It was hard to tell because it happened so fast. Something pulled and let go right away. If I had to guess, I'd say a fish, and a biggie."

I pulled my line up for a bait check. A lonesome hook dangled in the air after being mauled by an ornery brute.

"Maybe it was one of those elusive, big browns that Gramps and Pops used to talk about," Nub pondered as he looked through me.

"Probably." I looked skyward to my Maker, hoping for another chance. Nub offered me no consolation as he was back to fishing. "Well, we've only caught a few of them buggers over the years. They're just too finicky during the day. The last one caught was your three-pounder a few years ago up the right fork."

"Hold on there. Aren't you being a bit conservative?" Nub responded.

"Well, you only caught one."

"No, the weight, it was like four pounds. Actually, probably closer to five."

"Maybe three and some change if it wore a lead suit," I said while opening my worm can.

"That isn't right! It wouldn't fit into my creel. I carried that thing around like a pork shoulder for crying out loud. And it fought like a wild hyena. I ran up and down the stream battling through brush and boulders, and still landed it with my own hands."

Shaking my head in silence, I dug for the biggest worm in my can, hoping that juicy morsel would win the big trout over. Nub stood disappointed, trying to determine how his prized catch lost a pound a year since being caught.

I dressed my hook with a tailor's care and resumed fishing.

"You know, those big browns mainly feed in the evening, so they say. They're almost ghostly," I said in awe.

Nub rubbed his stubbly chin. "Sounds a lot like those big bucks we hunt every year. We know they're around, but we rarely get them."

"Yeah, they're an enigma too."

We gave our best effort to nab the cagey brown. We flossed the sides of the logs and branches with precision casts, looking for Mr. Big in every nook, but he proved too elusive.

Our endeavors weren't fruitless, however, as we caught a few smaller trout, including a chunky ten-inch brookie that I added to my creel. It was meaningful to get a keeper where the boys had already fished, for many moons ago Gramps caught a keeper after I had fished a hole, and he let me know it.

"Tony," he would say, "fish more thoroughly. Be more patient and read the water. When you finish a hole, nobody should want to fish behind you."

In other words, if you're doing something, then do it well. I took that to heart.

Nub and I crawled back up the bank in pursuit of the kids. We took one last look at the beautiful stretch of water we had just fished. Sometimes it's healthy to slow down and absorb the river from another vantage point, without fishing, without moving. Just look, listen, and savor the scene. A frozen moment can warm a soul.

Moments later we trekked the wood's edge, periodically peeking over the stream to locate the boys. They had put more distance between us while we re-fished their hole. The walk through that neck of the woods was particularly tough. A small, slippery ravine left a bruise on my backside, and some dense patches of alder and young pine left their mark on my cheek and forearm. Meanwhile, Nub was introduced to the forest floor after trying to straddle a huge log.

There weren't any glorious, patted down fisherman paths out there. It was tough and rugged wilderness. We blazed our own trails. Occasionally we'd steal some yards down a deer path, but that was it for help.

Our battle through the brush ended when I spotted the tops of two brimmed caps hovering over the stream. I bent away a few branches and stretched my neck for a better view.

"I see the boys. Let's head down there."

They turned towards us when they heard our boots thump down the clay bank. Alex was on the left fishing in shin-deep water, drifting in some slow current. His baseball cap was pulled low, breaking the sun's rays that blasted his upper body. Drew was at the river's edge, digging in his vest. A pack of gnats swirled in the sunshine a few feet above his head, but they were only spectators instead of diners. He left the gnats behind as he stepped on the sandbank and crunched towards us. Although he was tall for his age, he was still agile and coordinated.

"How she go, fellas?" Nub asked as he tried to read the expression on their faces.

"Pretty good," Drew said while grabbing his creel. A pair of greenish hazel eyes danced around under his ball cap. His thick, wavy hair was too much for the hat, which only partially covered a sea of sandy brown locks.

Alex felt the group's call, so he pulled in his bait and hooked it to the pole's base. An excited young fisherman slogged towards us with one hand carrying a pole and the other adjusting his creel, while his vest hung loosely over his worm can. His thin build accentuated the bulges of the equipment he carried.

"We caught several brookies and a brown in the last hole. We got three more right here," Drew said with arched eyebrows.

"Yeah, Drew caught two keeper brook trout and I got this one," Alex said. He opened his creel and revealed a hefty fifteen-inch brown that still dripped fish slime.

Nub eagerly stepped forward. "Where'd you get it?"

A bashful grin leaked from Alex's boyish face as he turned and pointed to his hot spot. "Right over there, under those two big logs."

"Did it put up a good fight?" Nub asked.

His brown eyes grew wide as he grabbed a breath to speak. "Oh yeah! I thought my line was going to bust there for a minute."

I walked to the river's edge and closely inspected the hole. It was a nice set-up with good shade, ample current, and dark olive water.

"Hey son, how'd you fish this? You threw your worm upstream and rode the current into the deep water under the logs?"

"Yep. It goes under there on its own." He removed his cap and swung it to trace his winning drift. A crop of short brown hair was momentarily exposed.

"Perfect! That's the way to do it. And no snags either?" I asked as I walked back.

"No. Not really." Alex plunked his cap back on his head.

"Lucky you!" I bent over and scanned his dandy trout. "Jeez, son, that's a great fish. As Gramps and Pops would say, that could be today's top banana. We don't get those biggies very often up here."

"That's for sure," Nub added. "You the man!"

Alex had more to say. "I caught a sucker in that hole right after the trout."

"Really?" I exclaimed with surprise. "Did you get rid of it?"

"Yeah. I threw it in the woods like you guys. It was pretty big too."

The sucker, or white sucker, is a bottom feeding fish that typically isn't targeted by sportsmen. Suckers were more plentiful in the slower moving waters of the Lower Flag, and when Gramps and Pops hooked one they gave them the heave-ho into the woods followed by a few Italian expletives. To them they were a nuisance and they ate trout eggs. It was unusual to catch a sucker above the Forks, but when we did, we followed the family practice.

Our attention shifted to Drew. He flipped open his creel and peered inside it. In short order, he gripped a slippery trout and lifted it for display.

Nub slid in for a closer look. "What you got in there?"

"I got this thirteen-incher over there," Drew said while pointing left to some dark water.

"Man, that's a real nice brookie!" Nub exclaimed.

The beautiful fish deserved maximum attention, so I closed in for a better look. Sure enough, the display piece exhibited vivid colors and an intricate design that were masterfully wrapped around a sleek profile.

"Wow, that's a dandy!" I said while giving Drew a light punch in the arm.

A smile blasted across his face.

Nub leaned over, tilting his head sideways. "Hey, there's a slight hook on its lower lip."

Drew lifted the fish higher and we all focused on the trout's lower jaw.

"Yeah, you're right Nub, there's the slightest turn right at the tip. That's pretty cool."

Alex broke his silence and lobbed a well-placed question. "What's with that hook anyway? Does it help them out somehow?"

"That's a good question," Nub responded. "Salmon get a hook when they are spawning."

"Oh yeah, I've seen that on T.V. before," Drew agreed.

"Actually, brook trout are in the salmon family," Nub stated.

I pinched my lips in thought. "You know, I read that somewhere. Maybe the hook lip makes sense then."

"Brookies spawn in the fall," Nub was quick to point out. "The hook has something to do with maturing and mating, probably a dominance thing like with a lot of animals."

Alex turned his attention towards Nub. "Uncle Nubby, is your well-developed butt chin a sign of your dominance?"

Drew and I got a good belly laugh from that remark.

Nub scratched his whiskers and mumbled "Yeah, yeah."

There's nothing like some spontaneous humor to liven up a trip.

10

Rings of Wisdom

We stood in a loose huddle and recollected ourselves. Now it was my turn to show them a thing or two.

"Hey boys, check this out." I pulled out the brook trout I had caught earlier. "See this beauty?"

They nodded inquisitively.

"Guess where I caught it?"

"Well, how should we know? We weren't fishing with you back there," they responded.

"That's true, but you might as well have."

"Huh?"

Now they were really intrigued.

"I caught it while standing in your boot tracks in the last hole."

"Oh, yeah . . . well, we caught some there too."

"So, maybe you left too early?"

They blurted out an uncomfortable "I guess so."

"I'm just reminding you guys to slow down. Take your time and enjoy it. We have all day you know."

Nub nodded in agreement as he stepped back and scanned the bank behind us.

"What's the matter Nubby, did you lose something?" I asked.

"No, not at all. I was thinking about those wild leeks that Gramps and Pops used to talk about. I've never found one."

"Well, don't feel bad. I've only found a few myself."

"Hey, Grandpa talked about taking a leak out here," Drew said in a half silly manner.

"Alright, wise guy," I responded matter-of-factly. "Besides, shouldn't you be leaving a leak instead of taking one?"

His eyebrows jumped, and I winked with humor.

"Anyway, a wild leek is a type of onion. They grow in late spring," I went on.

"What do they look like?" Drew asked after collecting himself.

"They kind of look like a garden onion. Their green tops are different though."

"Like how?"

"Well, they look like a set of rabbit ears," I said.

"Hmm. That's weird."

"Did you snack on them while you fished?" the kids asked.

"Nah, I don't remember doing that."

"So you just carried them around while you fished?" they asked.

"Well, yeah. I mean, we put them in our back vest pocket and cleaned them later." I reflected for a moment. "Gramps and Pops cut them up and sautéed them with the trout."

"Were they any good?" Drew wondered while he licked his chops.

"They were good stuff. They had a garlic flavor that was a bit different for an onion."

They had wonder in their eyes and they drifted off for a bit, tasting the words I had spoken.

"I tell you what, if we fish here in early June, we'll look for some."

We fastened our creels lids and headed upstream in single file with me in the lead. The river ahead was straight, shallow and clear for walking.

"Whoa, did you all see that?" I blurted out with my eyes fixed on the stream.

A jet-powered outline blasted past us in the water. With a few flicks of its tail, the darting figure swam downstream of us in a blur, leaving only a puff of dirt that quickly dissipated in the current.

"We just spooked a keeper," I lamented.

Alex and Drew missed the fleeting action, but Nub noticed it.

"Jeez, maybe a foot long," he said while he removed his hat and rubbed his noggin.

In the trees above, two squirrels initiated a series of loud chatters. Normally I relished the sounds of wildlife along the river, but in this case I wasn't so sure. Were the furry spectators passing a good time at our expense? Their scurrying broke some twigs loose, one of which bounced off my hat brim and cartwheeled into the water.

I held council with the troops. "Alright guys, we've been sent a message."

"Like what do you mean?" the kids asked.

"We're too fast and noisy," I said while putting my hand on my hip. "Alex, how about you and Drew hit the woods and walk for several minutes before you start fishing. Nub and I will stay in the stream."

The kids maneuvered their way up the right bank and tromped through the woods. Their profiles quickly turned into bustling green leaves that soon turned still.

We worked up the river and scouted for the spooked trout's hiding spot.

With a puzzled look I asked, "Where the heck was that fish hiding? There's no obvious cover in this area."

"Maybe it was crammed under a bank. They don't need much room to hide, you know."

"That's true. I wonder how many fish we walk by in a day. We think we got it figured out, but we're probably fooling ourselves. Nature humbles us again," I said, adjusting my cap for good measure.

Up ahead a swift, shallow run overrode a sandy bottom. The sandy areas had beautifully crafted ripples across their faces. Those features formed perpendicular to the current direction, as wavy bottom currents molded armies of sand grains into ridges. There was a field of them. I watched the stream slowly rebuild a crested ripple I had just stepped on. It reminded me of ants rebuilding a mound, minus the ants of course. The river gracefully played the role of an invisible sculptor.

Nub got ahead of me thanks to my daydreaming.

"What are you doing over there?" He looked back and asked.

I lifted my eyes while keeping my head down. "Ah, nothing really. Just looking at ripples in the sand. You know I like that kind of stuff."

"Yeah, I noticed them things. I just don't stop and stare at them like you," he heckled me.

The water was only ankle-deep, which challenged even the most seasoned trout fisherman's prowess to maintain quiet steps. I tiptoed closer to my brother who had slowed his pace.

"Hey look, there's that huge black spruce," he said while directing me with his eyes.

"Man, now that's a tree, Nubby!"

My brother stood stiff with a hand on his hip. "I remember that tree from before. I knew it was up here somewhere."

The majestic black spruce stood off to our right, where the woods met the stream bank. That tree had a presence, like a relic from an enchanted forest. It stood tall and pointed as it looked down upon us. It would have taken at least two people to wrap their arms around its sturdy base. A collection of roots exposed by the river's erosive force held firmly to the bank. Patches of green moss and lichen covered old man spruce's craggy brown hide and reminded me of age spots on an elderly person. I felt insignificant in the company of that tree, but it felt good to be minimized in its presence. If only that forest king could have spoken. I would have paid a pretty penny to learn from its rings of wisdom.

We stood side by side and gave the towering wooden statue one more look.

I lifted my cap and addressed an itch. "You know, this tree reminds me of those humongous willows down at the Forks."

Nub searched his memory. "Which ones again?"

"You know, when we park down by the Forks, we walk right by them. They're just before we hit the river. They have those super long, gangly branches that hang to the ground."

"Yeah, I think I remember," he said while he stared a hole through the spruce.

"For some reason they stand out to me. I picture them in front of a haunted house."

"Like on the Munsters?" Nub jokingly asked.

"Ha-haa. Yeah, like that. They're just cool trees."

Those flowing willows had an aura about them. They were sprawling beauties. Their bases were hidden behind their lush growth like Mardi Gras revelers behind their masks. I wasn't sure what to make of those long, stringy branches. They looked inviting, like a hug might be forthcoming. On the other hand, they looked daunting, like the trees might strangle me instead. Either way, I was fond of them.

11

Old Timers

My mention of the Forks got Nub thinking. "You know, that big hole at the Forks is weird," he blurted out.

"Like what do you mean?"

"Well, that hole always looks great. It's deep with good current, but we don't catch squat out of it." He switched his rod to the opposite hand in a fidgety way. "I mean, when was the last time we caught something out of that thing?"

"Hmmm, probably several years ago. Maybe a couple of rainbows." I paused for more ammo. "We don't fish it every trip you know. We probably won't get down there today either."

"Yeah, I get that, but for the number of times we've fished it there's been little production."

I analyzed the hole in my mind. "Maybe it's the sun. The hole is in the middle of the stream where the two rivers meet."

"True. Not much shade there," he rationalized. "Come to think, there isn't much cover there either."

"Then again, maybe it's overfished. There's always forked sticks stuck in the sand."

Nub grimaced. "Oh yeah, those things."

"Hey, you never know, we might need to use them one day."

"Hopefully I'm long gone before I have to prop my rod on a stick," Nub said out the side of his mouth.

I admired the gritty attitude.

My mind hovered over that oasis at the Forks. An overgrown fisherman's path connected a gravel parking lot to where the East and West Forks of the Flag joined hands. The path, although barely discernible, was a rarity along the Flag.

The old timers occasionally "camped" at the Forks and fished. We noticed the vestige of earlier fishermen in the form of boot prints and forked sticks that were plucked from nearby trees. Strands of broken fishing line sometimes hung from overhead limbs like tinsel. Once we found a broken cloth chair with wooden legs buried in the brushy bank.

I imagined the scene of those camped fishermen, where a laid-back pair of grayed anglers sat comfortably near each other, their chairs melting into the sand. Two propped poles were dormant while lazy lines arced downward and disappeared into the swirls of the circular hole. A slow-moving current swept by without a care in the world.

A small cooler with sandwiches and soft drinks sat nearby. The veteran anglers spoke in soft tones about the "good ole days," back when they walked and probed the river's runs and curves. Gentle hand waves helped accentuate their discussions. Passion glowed from their faces with each passing story. The stream applauded with soft gurgles and graced them with whiffs of cool air.

They watched their rod tips, not because they expected action, but because they were accustomed to doing so. They were still fishing after all. An old wicker creel rested between them along with a rusted worm can. Two old tattered fishing vests were folded over a log.

It was a portrait that Norman Rockwell might have depicted, where one moment whispered years of well-spent time. It was two friends, or possibly brothers, who came together to relive a lifetime of memories.

Who were those old anglers? Nobody I knew. Or perhaps it was a vision of the future, and I knew exactly who they were. If that's our fate, then so be it. It's best to embrace the thought of aging, it makes for a happier life.

Nub was ready to move, so he spoke up. "How about we stop jabbering about forked sticks and go get some fish?"

I snapped out of the fog. "Yeah, I suppose we should get moving." I paused for a moment. "You know, I was just thinking. Maybe hanging out at the Forks isn't all that bad."

Nub turned with a concerned look. "Like what do you mean? You want to go there now?"

I chuckled. "Nah, that's not what I meant." I dropped my head and made eye contact with the stream. "It's just that those old timers probably enjoy it there. Maybe they're trying for those big browns later in the evening."

"I guess. That's actually not a half-bad thought." Nub scratched his stubbly chin. "We might need a couple of cold longnecks if we did that."

"Absolutely!" I roared with a big grin. "And maybe even a few more than a couple!"

"I hope we're not turning into some softies," Nub mumbled as he led us upstream.

Neither one of us commented on that thought. We've talked before about why we still fished the Flag.

During my younger years, I visited the Flag for the obvious reason—to catch trout. I wanted a limit each trip. I was competitive about it, too. After Gramps passed away, I decided nobody would out-fish me on my "own" stream, and that's the way things went for many years.

As a teenager and young adult I fished with friends, with my family, and sometimes alone. I worked hard to hone my skills and elevate my game on the stream. I just flat out loved to stream fish, especially on the Flag. While camaraderie made the trips fun, my main goal was a heavy creel at day's end. I was too young to understand the deeper meaning of what unfolded with each trip. I was eager to take, but less willing to leave anything behind.

As I aged, my trips were only with family. I developed into a deeper fisherman, one with a soul for the area. The give and take became balanced. The stream gave me opportunity to play with its finned children like always, but in return, I left part of myself. I grew to admire not only the river, but also its surroundings. In the process, our family ties grew stronger.

My contemplative state ended when I noticed my partner pointing ahead.

"You spot something?" I asked.

"Yeah. There's a hole around the bend."

"Is there room for both of us?"

We nudged closer to the near bank.

"I think so. There's a long hole along that fallen spruce," Nub said.

I peered over his shoulder. "Over on the left bank?"

"Yeah."

"Looks pretty good alright. Hey, look further up," I said, directing with a head jerk.

A leafy elm tree lay across the river channel a few feet above the water. Its base intersected with the lower portion of the fallen spruce and formed an L-shape. A swift current flowed underneath the elm's base and later slowed as it passed the half-submerged spruce.

Nub squinted as he scanned under the elm. "I think that's a hole too."

"Go ahead and try it and I'll work below you."

We waded in knee-deep water to our target zone, with Nub positioning himself to work under the elm, while I looked to work the sluggish current below that paralleled the spruce. We lobbed our baits upstream and drifted the current down.

"I got a nibbler already," Nub whispered.

"My worm is just bumping off some snags."

Nub slowly shifted his pole across his body as he followed the drift downstream. His rod tap-danced intermittently to a trout's tango.

"You going to set the hook?" I asked quietly.

"It keeps letting go. Might be a smaller one."

I finished my unsuccessful drift and held my worm in the air while Nub worked his bait near me. Suddenly, he snapped his wrists.

"Finally," he said while his gear rattled. "Timing is everything."

Nub fought the fish while he looked around for a landing place.

"We don't have a sandbank," I said, stepping back to give him more room. "Give him the ole heave-ho into the brush if it has any size."

The battle was short lived and my partner opted to lift a nine-inch brook trout directly to him. A faint line of blood drizzled down its lower jaw, but it still seemed healthy and unfazed. The spunky fellow darted off to cover upon release.

"I could have used a net for that one," Nub noted while he bent down and cleaned his hands.

"Yeah, but you'd have to carry it with you all day." I prepped for another underhanded cast. "That would be a pain."

"Hey, how about that old trout fishing net that Gramps had."

I nodded slightly. "The one with the brown wooden handle?"

"Yep. It's the size of a racquetball racquet."

A subtle plop settled in the background as my worm tasted the drink.

"It's hanging in dad's garage I think."

"Did anybody ever use that thing?" Nub asked.

"Oh, I'm sure Gramps used it, but I never saw him with it," I answered.

"He probably quit using it after lugging it through the woods."

I didn't respond because my pole started to vibrate mid-drift. The trout was aggressive and it slammed my bait.

"Here we go," I grunted.

"Get it away from those pine branches," my partner advised.

"It wanted back in the cover, but I got it now."

We muddied the water as we maneuvered around during the action. My pole thumped to a rapid beat, but I kept my rod tip up and directed the trout towards me until it tired.

"Another nice brookie," I said. A beautiful eight-incher flipped in my grasp as I prepared to release it.

We let the current clear the cloudy water around our tracks, and then we tried our luck again.

"Look at that bite. Tick, tick, tick," he said under his breath as he verbally mimicked his rod motion.

"Sure sign of a little one, Nubbie."

He deftly avoided hooking the undersized trout and prepared for another drift, this time closer to the fallen pine.

"Now it's my turn," I said. "More little taps on the worm."

I set the hook to see the culprit. Sure enough, a fingerling was attached to my bait, but thankfully fell off at the water's surface.

"Did you see what that was?" I asked.

"Nah, it was hard to tell. Maybe a little brown, if I had to guess."

"Boy, you'd think there would be some bigger ones in here."

"No kidding, this is a nice hole."

"Oh well, we're still getting action," I said, trying to be positive.

A stretch of quiet passed between us before we both noticed the same thing.

"Hey, both of those downed trees are fresh," Nub mentioned.

"I was just wondering about that."

Nub hypothesized. "I was thinking wind, but I bet it was the spring runoff that took them out."

I looked hard at the base of both trees. "Yep. Both of them were rooted at the bank's edge. The river must have gotten real high."

"It sure did," Nub said. He pointed above our heads at some loose sticks and grass that hung off a branch from a rooted ash tree.

We both stared up while our lines drifted slowly across our bodies.

Nub eyeballed across the top of the bank and made an estimate. "That would have overflowed the bank."

"Hey, that makes good sense. Remember the sand in the woods before the last bend?"

"Oh yeah. There was a half foot of it in places."

The geologist in me kicked into gear. "That was from the river dumping its sediment load. The water loses speed over the bank and the sand grains drop out."

"Seems sensible enough."

My mind kept working. "So, how much snow did you guys get last winter?"

"A ton," he said disgustedly.

We both swung our worms upstream for another pass and continued our deductive discussion. "So, there you go. A ton of snowmelt helped cause flood conditions."

"Plus it rained a fair bit in April and May."

"Jeez. That's a bad combo."

He looked up again. "Man, it's just hard to believe it gets that high."

"Well, believe it. We see the signs. Actually, I fished once in early May when I was in college."

"And?"

"I didn't get squat. Maybe a couple." I paused and thought about that trip. "I went alone and was amazed at what the Flag looked like."

"Pretty bad, huh?"

"It was nasty! High, fast and full of brush and logs floating down the river."

"That's not good."

"It was dangerous. I fished off the bank and left early."

"Gramps and Pops always said that the holes changed each year," Nub said.

"Yes they did. A good spring cleaning does the trick alright!"

It was Mother Nature's version of a facelift.

12

Gander Mountain

*O*ur fishing action slowed to the pace of a clock's hour hand. We lifted our baits, hooked them to our poles in unison, and stepped towards the big leafy elm that blocked our path upstream. It was too low for us to slide under, yet too high and brushy for us to go over. We were forced to backtrack, but before we turned, a fleck of white caught our attention.

"Somebody's up ahead," Nub noted. He bent some branches aside and pushed his head forward. "It looks like Drew sitting on a log over the stream."

"What's he doing over there?"

"Hmmm. I guess fishing."

Drew straddled a pale-faced log that had long since lost its identity. Its smooth backbone spanned the stream's width and provided a natural bridge from one bank to the other. He was perched on the right edge and his feet dangled a few feet above shallow water. His rubber hip boots covered most of his suspended legs. A ball cap shielded his focused eyes and an oversized fishing vest hung casually over his torso. A background of green brush crowded his space while a slip of blue sky fought for exposure between mounds of tall canopy. He sat quiet and alert while carrying an aura of being content and peaceful. His arms were pitched forward as he worked his bait in the current before him.

River Pupil

There was a hopeful, natural innocence to the scene. The pure and simple element would have melted a mother's heart.

A few moments later Nub leaned back and casually said, "Well," which in our brotherly language meant, let's go.

We looked downstream. "Looks like we have to go backward to go forward," I said.

Nub dug around in his front vest pocket for a piece of beef jerky. "Yeah, that stinks. It's not the first time though."

"And probably not the last either," I sighed.

He tore off a piece of dried meat with his teeth and stuffed the remainder back in his vest. We waded side by side and felt for solid bottom, muddying the water ahead as we walked downstream.

"Where's Alex?" Nub wondered. He spoke from the side of his mouth while he clamped down on the jerky.

"Probably around the next bend." I pushed some brush aside as we looked for a low angled bank. "We asked them to stay together, so I'm sure he's close."

Nub found a good exit point and led us up a scarred bank. We passed by Drew's log, but he had already abandoned his post, so we walked in the woods long enough to leapfrog over the boys. Afterwards, we reentered the stream and traversed along a drenched gravel bed that gave way to some tumbling water and big logs.

"Hey Nubby, check it out up there."

A brief look was all he needed. "That's got to hold trout. Let's go in easy," he said.

We crept along the right bank and got within casting distance of the promising hole. A nagging sun warmed our backs and left its heated signature in the air around us. Some pesky mosquitoes danced in a waning breeze and tickled my face with false landings.

We stood together on a moist sandbar that held clumps of knee-high grasses dotted with ladybugs. The river was in spectacular form, imparting an eye-popping prism of color associated with the change in water depth across its face. In the shallows, a field of stones glistened through the water and mimicked a painter's palette, while an olive-colored river channel slanted and dove into the depths of midnight. Two logs angled into the pulsating flow; their branches antlered outward with rugged grace. The channel's back end released a corridor of bubbling current that poured generously into a deep pool. An overlooking bank drooled spring water and held piles of avalanched sediment at its base.

I cast my eyes to the heavens above and then back to the river shapes before me, and thanked God I was a trout fisherman.

"Hey Nub, this spot has that "Gander Mountain" look, wouldn't you say?" I said, expressing my thoughts.

"Yep. A perfect outdoor picture!"

A touching thought struck me. "You know Mom would really like it here. Knowing her, she'd have a pole in one hand and a paint brush in the other."

"That sounds about right."

Our mother loved the outdoors, which partnered well with her adventurous spirit. Now there was a lady who dressed and acted half her age, which was a compliment for an older person with grown kids. She visited the Flag a few times on our family trips and even caught a few. Even though she seldom fished with us, she was always part of the trip. Who else would wait at home with arms wide open, wanting to soak up the day's adventure through her sons' eyes and voices?

Although she enjoyed being a sportswoman, she truly loved music and art. I imagined her sitting on the bank with toes tapping, capturing the scene with rhythmic strokes of a brush. She was a fair-skinned lady with short reddish locks, thanks to her predominantly French ancestry. Her peppy personality and quick smile touched everyone she met. She not only lived her life, she lived it with a beat.

Being a person of great devotion, she'd toss all her talents and desires aside just to be with her family. That was the glue that bound us all together.

"So, talking about mom, I know she hasn't been feeling all that great, but she doesn't look too bad, huh?" I carried an upbeat tone with my question.

Nub was expressionless. "She looks alright, I guess. I mean, we see her off and on, so maybe we don't notice any changes."

"I just get concerned because of her family history, you know, with cancer and all. And mom isn't big on using medical doctors."

"Yeah, she's funny about the doctor thing," he said uncomfortably. "What all's in the family again?"

"I'm not totally sure—breast cancer, and either colon or ovarian or both. We probably should get that stuff straight at some point."

We fiddled with our equipment with those thoughts in mind. I removed a nicked-up worm from my hook and replaced it with a squirmy fresh one. We usually broke our night crawlers in half because they fit better on our small hooks, and they seemed to fit better in the trout's mouth too. Nub re-hooked his loosened bait and reached in his vest for a splash of bottled water. We weren't to be rushed.

I spoke quietly while my eyes absorbed the setting.

"You want to take the upper half under the logs, and I'll work the pool in the lower half?"

He agreed and we moved into place while pulling line from our reels. Their rough notes pierced the river's hum—a familiar and comforting sound to us. We eyed our worm's destinations and sent them looping in the air with underhanded pitches.

My worm rode a gentle current into the pool's edge, and I steered it away from a submerged branch that forked towards my drift.

Nub's worm was gobbled up by the current and pulled under the logs by its natural force. He kept a keen eye as his bait traversed the channel that was overshadowed by the logs.

A glance at my brother reminded me of days gone by when I stood in tandem with my grandfather, or at times, with my father. No words need be spoken when immersed in such a solemn setting, as peace and contentment proved to be an effective muzzle.

Nub had learned the nuances of this stream well over the years, and I happily counted him as my equal. He certainly looked the part, with a rugged build that was complemented by a near black mustache and a square chin. His defined jaw line was framed with a dark carpet of whiskers that would have made a lumberjack jealous.

Many years in his trade as a sheet metal foreman had created a pair of meaty hands. However, he held his pole and line much gentler than one would think. While his line of work toughened his frame, it didn't destroy his finesse on the stream. He worked his fishing pole in a fashion that reminded me of our father and grandfather. I took comfort in that.

A Cabela's cap with securely balanced sunglasses on its brim topped him off. The trout fishing gear, including Gramps' old worm can, matched nicely with his blue jeans and worn cotton shirt, while an occasional splat of tobacco juice rounded out his persona.

There are those who fish for bragging rights, where a trophy on the wall or a dazzling picture is their motivation. Others only go when the weather's perfect, or when they get a hot tip for a sure catch. Some simply show up because a friend dragged them out, or because they hoped to show off some new, splashy equipment. Of course, there are the partiers, who use fishing as a disguise for a good time.

My brother is none of those types. Instead, his trips are driven by passion, tradition, camaraderie, and a deep sense of appreciation for the outdoors. Oh sure, he relishes a nice catch, hopes for favorable weather, and passes a good time, but those things don't necessarily define his trips, they just happen in context.

When a guy gets excited about preparing for a trip, even though he's done it a hundred times, he's more than just a fisherman. When a guy enjoys a trip's back end, where he cleans and stores his equipment with the thoughtful patience of a German clockmaker, he's more than just an outdoorsman. No, that guy is a special weave. He's a traditionalist, an outdoor enthusiast. Stories are written about those types because their essence defines the wholesome nature of the sport.

I thought of my brother in that fashion, and realized that I matched shades of the same description. I mused upon his time-tested trout fishing list that we used before each trip. The folded, faded paper made our initial trip. How could that family manuscript not be appreciated, as years ago I had one of my own?

Nub's timing of being locked into the Flag was delayed versus my own, namely because Gramps passed away when Nub was ten. Although Nub started fishing at the age of eight, he only experienced a couple of trips with Gramps. He got more exposure during our family trips with Pops at the helm, but those trips were sporadic, although they did set the foundation for him at the Flag. He stayed connected to the trout by dabbling in small streams around the Duluth area. He stayed connected to the outdoors by becoming an avid sportsman through lake fishing, ice fishing, and duck, grouse and deer hunting.

When he was seventeen, we hooked up for a day at the Flag, and the rest is history. In short order, Nub became my best fishing partner and we've been going ever since. Fortunately, Nub settled permanently just outside Duluth, so our trips to the Flag continue whenever I visit the northland.

13

Silent Art

I was ushered out of my deep thoughts with a detonating "Feesh-On-Ralphie" from Nub. Sure enough, his rod bowed under thumping tension from a desperate trout on line's end.

"Hey, that's a good one!" I reveled.

"It's a fighter," he responded through tightened lips.

"Can you get it away from the logs?"

"I'm trying."

While he fought his fish, I nudged my bait through the semi-shaded pool. A few seconds later, a finned customer tugged my line and my pole took to life.

"I got one too!"

We were in the heat of battle, when in uncommon fashion, our poles went motionless. A building adrenaline rush swept past us like the stream's current.

I straightened up and adjusted my vest. "Dang, I lost him. I must have hooked him on the lip or something," I said with disgust. "Where's yours?"

Nub shook his head. "Gone. It must have bumped something underwater and jarred the hook loose." He stood disappointed.

That was part of the game. We took our bumps and bruises in stride.

"Well Nubby, if this was easy everybody would do it, right?"

"Right. I like feisty trout. It makes the outing a challenge."

I baited my hook and expected Nub to do the same, however, he didn't follow suit.

"What are you doing over there?" I asked.

His hand was motioning back and forth. "Sharpening my hook. I think this is Gramps' hook sharpener you know."

"Maybe, but I don't remember him using it. These hooks seem good enough."

"Well, this thing works. It can't hurt to use it."

"Probably so. Besides, you need all the help you can get anyway," I said with a humorous jab.

I yanked out some line and launched an underhanded pitch into the pool's center. The worm's cool bath was short-lived as my pole bent sharply to the weight of a second hungry trout. A sharp hook set thrust me into a full-fledged wrestling match with a stick of lightning, as sleek white flashes illuminated the water in front of me.

"Got another one!" I said. "This son-of-a-gun is a fighter."

"You didn't waste any time hooking that baby," Nub said.

"That's the way I roll!"

"Ah jeez, give me a break."

While the trout thrashed, a brilliant pinkish-red streak glistened from its side.

"Oh no, it's a rainbow," I muttered in a dejected tone. I banked the fish and measured it at thirteen-inches.

I held it up by its lip for a good look. The bright sun made the colors even more outstanding. "Man, look how thick and beautiful this trout is, but I can't keep it." I briefly wallowed in sorrow.

My partner took a few steps closer as I held the fish towards him. "What's the size limit again for those rainbows?" Nub asked.

"Like twenty-six inches I think. This one isn't even close. I'll let it go and catch it five years from now," I said with sarcasm.

I laid it gently back in the stream and tapped its side. The rainbow snapped to attention and darted under a log.

"Nice thinking. Make sure to bring a boat because it'll be living in the lake by then," Nub joked.

Nub went back to work under the logs while I baited my hook. In short order, he laid into another line-tightening trout.

"Right where the last one was," he said.

"You got a good spot there. But if you lose this one, the pro may have to move in," I prodded.

He pretended to ignore me.

He learned from the last fish and was quicker to yank his prey away from snag danger. A few hard-fought moments later, a water-slapping trout mingled in submerged gravel and was guided to dry land in short order.

"Watcha got there?" I asked, while flipping my worm to the pool's far edge, where it settled on bottom.

"A nice brown! Twelve inches or so."

"That's a keeper."

"Oh yeah. The bugger destroyed my worm too."

I jigged my pole to the side a few times. The motion worked up a trout's appetite and my rod danced like a string puppet.

"Yeah baby, another fighter!" I exclaimed after a hook set.

Nub rushed to put a worm on. "I'm going to get me another."

The fish bobbed and weaved in tight circles, so I rode it out, maneuvering around the pool until the trout rose to the surface. It helplessly swished a lazy tail as I pulled it towards me.

"A ten-and-a-half-inch brookie," I said.

"That'll keep," Nub encouraged.

"Huh. This one has a few scratches on its side. And a piece of its tail is gone."

"Maybe something big was after it," Nub said with hope.

We didn't need more encouragement to continue fishing, but the thought of a big one lurking below added extra zest to the experience. I introduced my latest catch to a fern lined basket and it thumped with disapproval.

We fished for a while longer and caught several more, but eventually the nibbles slowed. We were content to stay put and enjoy the simple but astounding beauty around us.

The day had grown warm, but I stood knee-deep in cool water, which balanced my body temperature. My eyes were drawn to a poplar branch that bobbled in the gurgling current. Its consistent pattern nearly dropped me into a hypnotic state. Another set of submerged poplar branches held their pale fingers above water and showcased a spider's delicate web work. Silent art.

A struggling June bug floated by en route to meet its maker, while a family of water bugs clung to dry land on the far bank's edge. A plate-sized eddy behind the logs held tight to a slow spinning pile of wooded debris. Above the eddy several cocoons fastened themselves to the log's crevassed bark. Perhaps this was nature's version of a busy street corner, but it was a spa to me.

A jagged forest line held desperate trees that jutted over the river; they fought with futility against the river's eventual capture. A safe distance back from the river's grasp stood a group of mature spruce trees that darkened the forest floor and filled the air with fresh pine scent.

Scattered clouds couldn't erase a fleeting shadow cast by a noisy crow. The black-winged creature called to the valley below, its voice echoing down the river fairway. Deep in the woods, a squirrel responded with resonating chatter.

Did I deserve to be there? I was truly humbled by the natural surroundings. However, simple pleasures in life are only pleasurable if noticed.

That type of natural experience grounds a person; it touches the human core. It's like a firm handshake with a salt-of-the-earth person, sincere and pure. Gone were the sights and sounds of the modern world. Here a mind could rest.

We came out of our spellbound states simultaneously and exchanged a glance while hooking our worms to our poles, which meant it was time to head upstream. It was worth its weight in gold to have a fishing partner on my wavelength.

"You ready to move on?" I asked while nudging forward.

"Yeah, let's get going."

We stopped and turned for one more look. What a hole!

14

A Good Coo-ntry!

*O*nward we went. Since fishing was so good, we traveled mainly by stream and fished anything that resembled a hole. We drifted the backside of boulders, poked under banks, probed under fallen trees, and worked pools big and small. Shaded areas held the most fish, but sunny spots also produced. Rapid runs of water also held trout as we plucked more than one from the river's riled mix. The trout were delightfully undisciplined and we couldn't have been happier for their wild ways.

"Hey Nub, is this a phenomenal day or what?" I asked, as we finished another action-packed hole.

"Yeah, it's been amazing. I think we've caught trout in every hole."

I studied our path forward. "Let's stay in the stream for a bit. The brush looks really thick."

Before starting our trek, we noticed a white, cigar-shaped object floating down the stream's midsection. It moved stiffly with the current and ricocheted off some sticks while continuing undaunted towards Superior's great holding tank.

"Looks like a dead trout, eh?" I said while pointing.

"Yep. Belly up. A small one, maybe six inches or so."

"I hate to see that." A look of concern shadowed my face. "I'm guessing the boys caused that."

"Probably. We'll have a chat with them."

"You know, we killed some too when we were younger," I reminded him.

My brother rearranged the tobacco in his mouth and spoke. "That's back when we didn't pay attention to that stuff. We had all those planted fish." He sent a shot of stained spit through the air.

"Yeah, that's true. Well, we're more aware of it now."

"Hey, sometimes they don't make it no matter what. A hook to the gill can do it in," Nub rationalized.

"Actually, this is the first one we've seen. The boys are doing well with that."

Waves reverberated off our hip boots as we resumed our venture upstream. The muffled crunch of gravel emanated from the soles of our boots. Not a word was spoken between us. An array of grasses, tangled brush and half-downed trees lined our pathway. A river-fresh smell saturated my nasal space and gave me a lift, while a strip of bright blue sky gave us hope that the day was long from over. There were times when an easy gait was like a good massage. That was one of those times.

After a short walk, we rounded a bend and bumped into the kids.

"There you are. Heck, we thought you were lost," we said half joking.

"So, how's it going guys?" I asked.

"Good. We're getting a lot of bites. We each have a few keepers," Alex replied.

"Any more biggies?" Nub inquired.

"No, but we got some nice brookies," Drew answered.

"We have about the same," Nub added.

I hated to change the subject. "Hey, are you two being careful releasing the trout?"

"Yeah," they responded together.

"We just saw one floating by," I said.

The kids looked at each other. Alex spoke up. "I had one swallow the hook. I pulled on it a few times and then cut the line."

"Was it bleeding?" I asked nicely.

"Not really. Well, yeah, some I guess."

"Just go easy with them. If they swallow it, cut them loose."

Nub piped up in a peppy voice. "Since we're all back together, let's keep our eyes peeled for a good place to eat lunch."

"Is everybody hungry?" I asked.

I was immediately drowned in a trio of positive remarks, along with a few snorts and grunts. We had burned a lot of calories up to that point.

Selecting a lunch spot was a fairly serious matter. I'm convinced that all complete trout streams come with specially designed lunch spots, sort of like wayside rests along highways. Nub and I were the primary lunch spot finders due to our vast experience in such matters.

After a short jaunt through the woods, Nub pointed upstream to a shaded stretch. "Take a look up there."

"That looks good. Let's check it out."

We hit the stream on a mission and landed in lunch central.

"Well, what do you think?" Nub asked.

"I'm in. It's got all the key ingredients, like that big log and some huge rocks. It's nice and shady here, too. And listen to that water gurgling. Man, that'll put me to sleep. This place has the ambiance of a ritzy hotel for crying out loud!"

Nub peered at the set up. "That big log is perfect. It's just the right height. I don't like my feet dangling, you know."

I gave a thumbs-up and we called the boys to join us.

Shortly afterwards, they ambled through the woods like two hungry bear cubs. They quickly joined us and unpacked their food with busy hands.

Above us, several tufts of cauliflower clouds crowded together and threatened to cast some shade amid a gorgeous day. A northwest breeze skimmed across Lake Superior and worked its way through the wooded landscape, drying our light sweat.

I stared at the smorgasbord around me, thinking about how gratifying it would be to transfer weight off my back and into my stomach. What should I eat first? There was an apple, some pickles, and a few pieces of beef jerky. There were crackers that paired nicely with pieces of Asiago cheese. A Nut Goodie bar laid nearby while a bottle of water stood guard over the layout. But the star of the show was the homemade sandwich.

We had prepared our sandwiches the morning of our trip so they pegged out the freshness meter. A soft white hoagie bun was lightly buttered and smeared with honey Dijon mustard. The hoagie held thin slices of spiced Italian ham called capicola, and additional slices of smoked turkey and genoa salami. The meats were capped with some fontinella and provolone cheese. Sliced homegrown tomatoes and mounds of leaf lettuce picked from Nub's garden added some fresh flavor. Luscious chunks of red pepper marinated in olive oil, vinegar, herbs and spices were added too. The juicy peppers were religiously added to the sandwich during lunch, and not before, as we didn't want soggy bread.

The beasty sandwich was my first target, so I wrestled it out of the Ziploc bag. My first bite was met with resistance, as my upper gum smashed into a wall of deli magnificence. Thankfully, as I pulled back, I knocked a piece of capicola loose and slurped it up. I took an embarrassing glance around, and hoped nobody witnessed my feeble attempt.

I sat for a second with a fleck of honey mustard on my chin, and prepared for another dive in. I squeezed the bread with more force and was rewarded with a flavor-charged mouthful. I continued my onslaught with deep satisfaction. What more could I want, as I sat over my favorite trout stream with a family of fishermen? I polished off my meal with honey mustard stains on my cheeks and seasoned olive oil and pickle juice dribbles on my whiskers. Wow! As Gramps would say in his Italian-slanted stream lingo, this is a good coo-ntry!

Our lunch extravaganza was nearing the end when Alex spoke up.

"Uncle Nub, what's with these Nut Goodie bars? The only time we eat these things is when we're trout fishing."

Nub glanced at me before he answered. "That started with Pops."

I followed up. "Yep, Pops usually had Nut Goodie bars on his trips—for years I'd say."

Drew gave me a perplexed look. "Did you guys eat lunch while you fished?"

"Funny you should ask. Your grandpa and great grandpa usually just snacked when they fished. They had their bigger meal at the wayside rest by Lake Superior."

"I know that spot," Drew responded.

"We'll stop there on our way back and have a snack. Maybe we'll have our rock throwing contest too," I said.

"Did you guys throw rocks, too?" Alex asked.

I laughed at the thought. "What, the older guys throwing rocks? Now that's funny!"

Nubby chimed in, "No, the rock throwing contest officially belongs to our group. Never mind us older guys both have bad shoulders. We're staying with it."

Drew probed deeper about lunch timing. "Well, why do we eat a lunch on the stream when you didn't before?"

I tried to be serious. "Ahh, it's related to a genetic defect of mine."

Drew looked worried. "Huh?"

I held back a grin and answered, "I was born human but I eat like a horse! I need a big meal sooner versus later out here."

Drew lightened up and a round of smiles laced the group as we packed up.

15

Honey Hole

We departed our "wayside rest" in single file up the bank, with me leading the way. My lanky frame provided me good leverage for using tree trunks to pull myself up the slippery slope. After clearing a few branches from my face, I assisted the others to higher ground.

The forest threw its typical temper tantrum while we stumbled through its tangled hair. A group of waist-high ferns wrapped around my legs and tripped me. Several yards later, the long arm of an aspen lodged in my creel strap and jerked me around such that I suddenly faced my crew.

"What's the matter?" Nub looked confused.

I was a bit frustrated, having felt like a mere pawn on the forest's chessboard. "These dang tree branches are driving me nuts. Help me get this bugger out of my gear. The thing whipped me around."

"Maybe you need to toughen up some," he poked.

"Huh! I'm blazing the trail. A lesser man would have crumbled hours ago."

"Yeah, yeah," my brother mumbled as he freed me.

The boys patiently looked on, waiting for the train to get moving.

We continued our march through a group of fine smelling cedars, only to have our path blocked by a deadfall that held a lumpy brown pile of animal dung.

"What do you think, Nubby? A black bear maybe?" I said while pointing.

"Yep. Looks like he's been busy with the berries."

"That's a weird place for a bear to take a dump," I noted.

"Hey! When you got to go, you got to go!" Nub joked.

We picked up the pace and distanced ourselves from the bear sign, appreciating the fact that we haven't encountered bears in past trips. After rounding another bend, we entered back into the water and encouraged the boys to lead us.

Moments later, Drew pointed upstream to where the river elbowed and lost itself beyond placid waters. "That might be good up there," he said with hushed enthusiasm.

Alex chimed in, "Yeah, it's got dark water."

Nub and I acknowledged the boys for having read the water up ahead, as Gramps had taught us.

The four of us held tight to the left bank, concealed by its foliage. We pushed away the overhanging bushes with disregard until we noticed the red jewels hanging off some leafy twine. Yeah baby—wild raspberries! The gems nearly bumped off my forehead, so I plucked a few of the soft fruits and tasted their sweetness. Wild raspberries are a gifted food, just crazy with flavor. A hovering bumblebee agreed.

Our slow-moving wake dissipated against the vegetated wall and was rendered silent, masking our movements as we walked in single file. The sound of boots in water changed to boots on sand as we reached a barren point bar that laced the inside portion of the river's curve. The boys kept a low profile and moved to work the upper half of the hole. Nub and I stayed below.

That hole held a considerable volume of dark water and a meager current hardly disturbed it. An array of bushes shaded its back flank, while the sun's rays stabbed at a generous frontal area. The river's bottom was relatively free of debris, at least to a fisherman's eye. If ever a stretch of stream smelled like fish, like fish to be caught, that one surely did.

We all flipped our worms into the honey hole. The boys covered the shaded back end, while Nub and I worked the front.

"Check out the boys," I whispered to Nub amid plops in the background.

He angled his eyes. "Yeah, this is good stuff."

"Pops would get a kick out of seeing these two hover over this hole like hawks."

"We'll have to tell him about it when we get back," Nub said.

Immediately Drew's rod tip stammered, and then Alex's pole followed suit with its own tap dance. They timed their bites perfectly with successful hook sets, and then stepped away from each other for more room, showing some natural fish-fighting abilities.

"The boys got a Double Dincau going!" I said.

Both boys nicely fought their fish, keeping their rod tips up and countering the trout's every move. After a skillful show, they landed them in the sandbank, coating them with grains. They shook ever so slightly while unhooking their catch, looking like seasoned fishermen with their hands doused in fish slime and worm juice.

"Are they keepers?" Nub asked while the kids scrambled to grab their tape measures.

"Yep! Looks like they're around eleven inches," the kids echoed with excited voices.

Is there anything better than watching two youngsters wrapped into an action-packed fishing experience?

"Are they brookies?" I asked.

"I think so. It's got the squiggly lines on its back and the white tipped fins," Alex answered in an adrenaline rush.

Drew nodded in agreement.

"That a way boys, that a way!" I called with a blast of pride.

My worm sat on a soft bottom based on my trout fisherman's feel, so I nudged it with a few light jerks. Shortly thereafter, the tap-tap-tap of a trout nibble transmitted through my line. I wasn't versed in Morse code, but I read that signal. Wham! I set the hook and laid into a solid fish. My dormant line grew legs and ran downstream towards faster water. I steered it away from the current and battled my quarry until it played itself out. It swished lazily back and forth while being ushered onshore. In the background, the boys' trout thumped in their creels.

"Hey. Here's the first brown from this hole," I said while showing the trout's profile so they could see a smattering of dots on its side.

"Is it going to keep?" Nub asked.

"Nah, it's maybe ten inches, but I'm going to let it go. I only need a few more keepers."

I released it into the cold water and it sat near the stream bottom, reacquainting itself with its environment. I touched its tail and it took off.

I straightened up and seized an obvious heckling opportunity.

"What's the matter, Nubby? Lost your touch?"

The boys' poles bounced again.

Nub expressed his mounting alarm. "Man, what's going on here?"

"Well, try moving to the left a hair. And pull your hat down a smidge," I needled him.

He didn't answer. Instead, a blast of wind rushed from his nostrils, which was followed by one of those "give me a break" looks.

"Hey, I was just trying to help," I said with a smirk.

In my haughtiness, I dropped my guard and made an amateur mistake by re-baiting while looking elsewhere, and the hook found my finger.

"Ouch! Dang it anyway," I yelped.

My brother looked my way. "Hey, keep it down. What the heck are you doing over there?"

"Ahh, the hook got me."

"Putting on a worm?"

"Yeah."

"Jeez, you must be getting old and losing your eyesight."

"Nah, I wasn't paying attention."

"Yeah, right," Nub shot back.

"Hey, I'm not that old. You'll be crossing into your forties soon enough, pal."

"Okay, old man," he softly replied.

"Well, I'm not getting any younger waiting for you to catch a fish in this hole."

Our brotherly banter was interrupted by a splash. Drew had another one and he leaned back to show the scrappy trout who was boss. It wasn't often that we worm fishermen battled a leaping trout, so when a leaper was upon us, we took note.

"Hey, look at that thing jump!" Nub stated.

Drew backed up on the sandbank hoping to land the fish.

"And again! Look at it go!" I added.

His fish stayed visibly high in the water column.

"Hey Alex, you watching this?" I asked.

He was tending to his own business, as he had hooked another. His pole carried a steady rhythm to the trout's beat.

"Hey, Nub. Look at Alex, too. Jeez, another Double Dincau!"

The boys both landed nine-inch brook trout and released them in short order. Meanwhile, I hooked another one. The feisty trout cut angles in the water and offered me a wonderful little ride, but it soon tired and cried uncle to its master. I gave the medium-sized brookie a good look and sent it back home.

Things were really heating up, as the natives were acting especially fearless and greedy. A drop of the worm caused a free-for-all, an aquatic bar room brawl by fishermen standards—a behavior totally acceptable when pole is in hand.

At this point, Nub had the hole to himself. The rest of us looked on while we dug in our worm cans. Finally, his pole took to life.

"You got something there?" I whispered.

"It's a nibbler."

"Any weight to him?"

"It's hard to tell. It's touch and go—kind of messing with my worm."

Finally, a decisive bite convinced Nub to set the hook. Bam! A fisherman and pole took to life. Nub took advantage of the open space and expertly jousted with his prey. The trout ran for a root-laden bank, but Nub read the move and steered him back to open water, and eventually brought him in. Shortly afterwards, a fine brookie flipped its tail, trying to escape my brother's grip.

"What do you think?" I asked.

"Ahh, it's a nice one, but probably not big enough to keep. Great colors on the thing, though."

"Sometimes that's worth more than weight in the creel," I said with some deep thought.

Nub's trout had swallowed the hook and a streak of crimson flowed from its gills. He cut the line and revived the trout for release. Drew had his own issues, as he untangled a mess of line at his rod tip. They both stepped back and rested their reels on a log while they worked. Alex and I resumed fishing, but the pace had slowed. Both of our lines carried a lazy arc over the water's surface.

I sensed something special while watching the profile of my son who stood alongside me. My own image was resurrected in a touching way. Why was it more obvious now than ever before? He resembled me at that age, with a lean frame, brown eyes, thick dark hair and a longer face. But that wasn't it. The physical similarity enhanced the image, but there was something deeper. Maybe because he was decked out in trout gear and stood over our family stream. The peace and solitude out there magnified our father-son moments. As a youngster in a short-sleeved shirt and a baseball cap pulled low, he didn't just go through the motions, but instead showed passion for the art. He was much like me in that manner. He worked his line like someone with more experience. It came naturally to him, and I couldn't help but soulfully stare. Perhaps my elders had a similar feeling when they fished with me years ago.

It dawned on me that another puzzle piece slipped into place. Having fished this stream with my family, particularly my son, allowed me to reconnect. I was reminded of who I was and who I grew to be. My inner self was revealed in a manner that couldn't take place in any other setting.

16

Four is Fun

"**H**ey, Dad. Ahh, Dad!" Alex called.

"Huh. What? What's the matter?"

"Nothing. What are you looking at?"

"Oh, well, I was just thinking," I said slowly.

"About what?"

I wasn't about to recite the fatherly drivel that had just passed through my mind. However, I had another observation. "Well, you're the only lefty fisherman that I've seen out here."

"I guess. The main thing is that I'm still catching trout."

"Yeah, you're learning well—both you and Drew."

Since the action had slowed, I opted for an underhanded pitch towards a fallen tree. Unfortunately, my hook and worm caught a limb and never found water. Both sinkers carried plenty of momentum and wrapped around the branch for good measure. What a mess.

I stood stiff in displeasure.

Nub and Drew lifted their heads as they headed back to dip their lines.

"Hey, nice cast," Nub prodded.

"Yeah, yeah. I missed my mark."

"Obviously. Good luck with that one," he said sarcastically.

Gritting my teeth and cringing, I snapped the line with a strong tug; it sounded like some type of supersonic slingshot—hardly music to a fisherman's ears. After my line went limp, I peeked towards the crime scene and watched the branch bobble back and forth in mocking fashion. The flexible limb held tight to my tackle and waved it around like a Mardi Gras float rider taunting the crowd with a hand full of beads. What's a fisherman to do?

We took our lumps in stride. Not every move was the right one, but that's the realism of life anyway. We always rebounded from the mishaps and kept going.

We got back to business and flipped our worms into untapped portions of the hole, hoping to lure more trout. We were rewarded handsomely to the tune of a Quadruple Dincau! All four of us hooked trout; it was unprecedented! Our rod tips popped back and forth while our lines zipped through the water with electric zest. It was really something to see four fishermen lined up on a river sandbar in the heat of battle. We skillfully jostled for position, and after some close calls, eventually landed the mini torpedoes without tangling our lines.

"How about that action, huh guys?" I asked while we released the trout.

"That was cool!" the kids fired off.

"Yeah, that was really something," Nub said enthusiastically. "That had to be a first—catching four trout at the same time."

"Agreed," I quickly replied. "Of course, we rarely fish four to a hole. But still, that was pretty amazing."

Everybody lost their bait on that go around, so new chunks of worm met each angler's hook. Nub and I picked up a few more brookies and a brown, and the boys added a few more trout as well. Finally, the "honey hole" ran out of steam and had nothing left to offer but simple beauty.

"Well fellas," Nub piped up, "I think this hole is finished."

The boys agreed, as their body language suggested they were ready to move on.

"How many did we pull out of here?" I wondered.

Drew and Alex looked at each other and guessed, "Maybe fifteen or so."

I strutted around amidst all the talk. "Guys, in all my years on this stream, nobody ever caught this many trout from one hole. We set a record here!" I proudly declared.

Nub initiated a round of loud-slapping high-fives.

"By the way, how's everybody doing for worms?" Nub asked.

The boys flipped their lids and took careful inventory.

"I have plenty," Drew said.

Alex scrunched his eyebrows as he dug around in his worm can.

He lifted his head and said, "I don't get it. There was a bunch in here a while ago."

I chimed in, "I should have reminded you about that old green worm can. The lid flips open too easy. I bet there are some worms back there celebrating their freedom."

Drew gave a small glob of worms to his hard luck partner.

Nub and I have questioned whether we should part ways with Gramps' original worm can. I used that can often during my younger years. Its many rust-filled scratches and minor dents were a testament to the rugged trails it had traveled while strapped to my side. On second thought, it's been a trusty companion and I wasn't so sure about retiring that baby. Perhaps that was a decision for another day.

While Nub cast a satisfied look into his bait box, I reached for my left hip, rotated the can and flipped the lid. I poked around inside the container, which was slightly smaller than a pop can. I had a good supply. They were still perky and knotted in a loose ball peppered with bits of earth and moist newspaper.

I flicked a few pieces of dirt off my fingertips and looked around. "Well fellas, ready to head out?"

Nub announced a plan. "Boys, how about you jump in the woods and head up?" He glanced at me. "We'll stay in the stream."

"Aww," they moaned. "Why do we always hit the woods?"

"You are subordinates. Remember?" Nub said, ribbing them. "The young guys always hit the woods."

I chuckled softly and unzipped my vest. Our banter afforded me time to grab a water bottle from my back vest pocket and quench a lingering thirst from lunch. The boys had learned from our past discussions not to argue any further, so they scampered up the bank and disappeared into the woods. Their quest for more trout action provided fuel for their swift departure.

"Remember when we were that young?" I said, as I put my vest back on.

"Sort of."

"I mean, like we couldn't wait to fish."

"Yeah. It was the only thing that mattered at the time."

I nodded. "The world could have been ending, but that wouldn't have stopped us." I lifted my hat and wiped a thin film of sweat from my forehead.

Nub slid his sunglasses over his eyes. "No problems and no worries," he said while stuffing a fresh pinch of chewing tobacco into a bulging lower lip.

And with that, we started upstream at a pace that fit our age. While I no longer fished with the insatiable desire of a youngster, I still enjoyed it. However, I was reminded of a healthy addiction that accompanied our stream time, which was the carefree, no worries atmosphere.

Our two figures passed through a gravel-carpeted straightaway that was walled with alder growth. The stream was shallow through that shady stretch, and the current bounced off our boots. We scanned under the root-infested banks, but nothing of interest caught our eyes. Finally, out of nothing better to do, I flipped my worm towards the left bank and let it carry downstream.

"You got a hole there?" Nub asked as he slowed his stride.

"Not really, just checking it out. You never know."

Two drifts later my rod tip broke rhythm from the gravel's cadence and bent downward towards a scrappy little brookie. "Hey, look at this!"

"Huh. Those buggers are everywhere!" Nub said as he tossed his worm towards the opposite bank.

One of Pops' old sayings held true—you can't catch a fish unless your line's in the water.

17

An Early Easter

We flipped our worms along the banks as we walked with patience. The trout were sparse in the remainder of the straightaway due to the shallow water.

That portion of stream carried a focused version of the day's gentle breeze. Apparently, the bordering alder growth helped form a natural wind tunnel; the funneled air scraped the moist banks and dispersed a light, earthy aroma. The stream's acoustics softly echoed around us. I was reminded yet again that trout fishing offered more than just hooking fish.

At the end of the shaded straightaway the sun's heavy presence awaited our arrival. Although I enjoyed the walk through the tunnel-like spa, I was anxious to find the next hole.

"There's a gravel island," Nub stated as he pointed upstream.

I scanned its edges. "There might be some holes on either side."

We trudged closer and pulled our brims closer to our eyes. The island held a dusting of grasses that grew from a rocky foundation. And what a rocky foundation it was! The island was full of rocks of all sizes, shapes and colors—a geologist's playground for sure.

Nub was drawn to the left where some fast water cut into a bank choked with sticks and roots. On the other hand, the rocks grabbed my eyes. It was a tough call for me to delay fishing, but I figured the holes weren't going anywhere. I bent over and handled a fist-sized, maroon colored sandstone. I felt its coarse texture and then put it aside for a piece of multi-colored granite. That held my attention for a few seconds until I spotted a nice chunk of slate. I was a kid among Easter eggs!

"Hey Nubby, look at these things," I said while holding up the slate.

He turned half way and continued to fish. "More rocks?"

"Well, yeah. But this is a really good spot. There's a ton of variety."

"Just let me know if you find a big agate."

The Lake Superior Agate is a prized stone and is often polished and sold at rock stores. Its wavy bands of multicolored silica attract even the most casual observer. Gravel-sized agates are not unusual to find, but larger ones are tough to locate.

"Sure," I responded with my head down.

I lost my brother's attention as he turned and started another drift.

A well-rounded piece of volcanic basalt called to me. I dropped the slate and held up my new find. "Hey, did you know these babies are over a billion years old?"

Nub only afforded me a glance. "Looks like a black rock."

That was a bit disheartening. I shook it off and moved to an area where some rocks were stuck in hardened clay. "Wow! This can't be!" I called to Nub.

"Now what?" He clearly wished that I had never stumbled upon the cornucopia of stones.

"Hold on, yeah, I think this is really it."

"What the heck are you mumbling about?"

By this time I had disrupted his fishing. He held his worm in the air and looked me over to ensure I hadn't lost my wits.

"An armored mud ball!" I said while examining the specimen.

"An armor of what? Is that some kind of agate?"

"Oh no. Not at all. You got to come over here."

"You're lucky I wasn't getting anything." He drew in his slack, hooked his worm to his pole, and walked over stiff-legged.

"Do you remember the one I found a few years ago? It was the size of my thumb but it was lithified. It was a real rock," I explained.

"I guess, sort of."

"Well, this is incredible, but I found a present day version!"

He stepped near me with a confused look. "You need to start speaking some English here or I'm heading upstream."

An armored mud ball is a geologic term for a clay ball that has small pieces of rock stuck to its outer body. It is appropriately named. It forms in rivers during periods of flooding and strong water flow. Highly erosive currents literally peel off patches of clay from the stream's bed and banks, rolling them into balls. During that process, the clay balls roll over small rocks, which become glued to the sticky body.

I held out the egg-shaped mud ball that fit neatly in my hand. "Look. We studied these in school."

"Hmmm. Kind of odd. So what does it mean again?"

"That a flood came through here and rolled the mud ball over the stones." I squeezed the clay ball. "Look, it's still soft. It probably formed this spring."

Nub's mind kicked into gear. "Hey, that jives with what we saw earlier."

"You mean the sticks and grass way above the stream and the fresh sand in the woods?"

"Yeah. It all points to big time flooding."

"It probably explains some of these nice gouged out holes we're seeing too." I was feeling pretty good about myself. "See, I haven't lost my mind."

"That's still debatable," he said while starting upstream. "You going to keep that thing?"

"I'd like to, but it's too soft."

Moments later, the armored mud ball rejoined its stony companions on the ground and I was back to fishing.

Nub worked further up the left side while I stood over a sheet of rapids that ran underneath a long row of bushes. The hole looked good from a distance, but that was a mirage. Up close, it was a tangled mess—a snag waiting to happen.

More scouting and a few chin rubs bolstered my courage to

attempt a side-winded pitch beneath the overgrowth. That technique was my only resort given the layout. The worm traveled only a foot before it banged off the jaws of a leafy branch and plopped into the current. In seconds, the bait shot downstream and out from cover where it tumbled into shallow water and was left in broad daylight. That wasn't good. Even if a fish struck under the cover, I'd have trouble setting the hook. My years of experience pushed me towards abandoning the hole.

I straightened up, gave the worm a pendulum swing back to me, and latched the hook. My eyes wandered back to the rocks. That was quite a collection the glacier deposited. Stones from northern Wisconsin, northern Minnesota, and well into Canada were gathered, carried and dropped as one happy family. I got a flavor of the region's geology by walking just thirty feet. Now that was cool!

My connection with the earth was a genetic thing. Before my tenth birthday, I began picking agates from a school parking lot next to our house. My efforts filled two coffee cans over the years. Occasionally a friend accompanied me, but usually I scoured the gravel lot alone. Being a "rock nerd" didn't come without some hard knocks though. Most people didn't understand my passion, but it didn't matter—it was my calling, and I loved it. I also loved trout fishing, so my time on the Flag was a perfect match of two passions for me.

A loud crack put me back into trout fishing mode. Nub had busted a small tree as he worked around his hole.

"You alright," I yelled.

"Oh yeah. Just stepped on a big branch," he hollered back amid the background sounds of rushing water.

I waved off a few mosquitoes and called back. "I'm going to try this little pool over here."

After side-hurdling a deadfall, I stood at the lower lip of a secluded pool. It was fed by a riffle of current that chattered over some polished rocks. My instincts were to immediately begin fishing, but I held back. Sometimes just the anticipation of being at a good spot was rewarding. An overhanging tree cuddled my right side while a boulder stood solid on my left. I felt comfortably invisible, like a human vapor.

A minute later my worm flew upstream and landed softly in the riffles that tickled the pool's far end. I nudged the bait along a rough bottom, aided by a tendril of current. Halfway through the drift a line-tightening trout introduced itself, and it felt my response via a firm hook set. In an instant, the pool's serene surface erupted from the struggles of a thrashing trout and I reacted accordingly, holding tight to my pole while enjoying the fracas. A few minutes later I landed a potential keeper, except the roulette wheel landed on a rainbow. I gazed at the vivid splash of crimson that traced its side, and then reluctantly released it back into the stream.

Subsequent pitches yielded few results, but it really didn't matter at that point. After several hours on the stream, I felt in rhythm with the river. It was like that first bike ride after a long, snowy winter. It was a bit awkward at first, but as the day progressed, my motions felt smoother and more natural. I sensed a real belonging here, a real sense of peace.

A trout stream is an uncanny place, where a fisherman can lose himself amid the action, and yet, be just as lost amid the opposite, where sweet sounds and cleansing sights charm the unsuspecting.

18

Payday

I departed from the little oasis and hit the woods to catch Nub, who had moved further upstream. A minute later, I stumbled out from the forest's gnarled grasp and landed loudly at the stream's edge. Nub was precariously hunched over in thigh deep water.

"Hey, how's it going?" I asked.

"Jeez, I thought a herd of elephants showed up."

"I tripped coming in. You hung up?" I questioned the obvious.

"Oh yeah, for the second time. I had a nice one on earlier."

"You get it?"

"No, it fell off right away. I tried for it again but got snagged. Broke my line that time."

I walked closer to help. "In that same hole?"

"Yep. Now I'm hung up—again, but I don't want to bust the line."

"Well, the hole's shot now," I said.

"I tried for a while, but I couldn't get him to bite. Figured I had enough here anyway."

He was mired in a nasty snag. He tried all the tricks to free his hook, including a few boot kicks. The last resort was to roll up a sleeve and try it by hand, which is what he was doing.

I stood in rushing water just behind him. "You need a hand?"

While I spoke, he came up with his worm, sinkers, and line intact. I grabbed his elbow and pulled him from the drink.

"That was lucky," I said as we both stepped back on dry ground.

"Maybe for you. You got to know what you're doing."

I shook my head. "Give me a break. If I didn't pull your sorry hide out of there, you'd be floating downstream."

"Huh! Maybe doing a leisurely backstroke."

"Really?" I laughed at the thought.

We recollected ourselves and slogged upstream, updating each other.

"How'd you end up doing?" Nub asked as he looked ahead for another hole.

"I let go a nice rainbow. Got it from that little pool."

"Nothing from the rapids with all the brush?" Nub asked.

"No. Hardly tried it. Couldn't get my worm in there."

"Hmmm. That looked pretty good too."

"What about you, anything?" I asked.

"Got a few decent brookies before that last hole. I kept one."

We came to a bend with steeply set banks, where some logs were strewn in dark water. A lazy current tickled their sides and overrode a clay-rich bottom.

I planted myself upstream of Nub in shin-deep water. Two boulders lay between us with their humped backs barely breaking the water's surface. Strings of dark green algae clung to the boulder's perimeters and moved at the current's every whim.

We started our drifts, but one attempt after another yielded nothing but some light nibbles. We nitpicked around some drowning branches with no luck.

After several minutes, I spoke up. "This is weird. Not a thing."

"These holes look decent too. We've been catching them out of places worse than this."

The Flag, in uncommon fashion for the day, was mocking us.

In desperation, I moved two steps into the river to better reach the opposite bank. In doing so, a rust-colored cloud emanated from my boots and was molded into the shape of a large comma by an underlying eddy. Unfortunately, the dirty cloud unexpectedly went downstream through Nub's hole. That was a severe breach of etiquette by trout fishermen standards. Nub lifted his head slowly and gave me a twisted glance.

"Oops," I said.

"Oops? Come on, give me a break."

I lifted my cap and roughed up my hair. "Well, who could have predicted that?"

"Maybe if you weren't fiddling with that beaver pelt on your head it wouldn't have happened."

"What! I can't believe you're even going there—Mr. Potato Head. Besides, my hair's got nothing to do with this."

I caught him off guard with that one. He was tattooed with that gem at our deer shack.

"I guess I got Ido's thin hair," he said while rubbing his head.

"Yeah, and I got Pops' thick mop."

"I probably lost some from Pops' army issue bug dope when we were kids," he said as he tried to justify his thinning crop.

"Well, I used that stuff too. It was strong, I'll give you that."

"Strong? It was like 110% DEET. I probably went half-bald at ten because of that junk."

"It worked well though," I recalled.

"I think the cans were solid green. You couldn't dent them with a hammer. Why in the world did we use that stuff?"

I had a quick reply. "For the same reason we used government cheese and powdered milk. The price was right."

A hearty chuckle erupted from Nub's diaphragm. "Remember that cheese block? It weighed like ten pounds!"

"Yeah, and we couldn't find a knife strong enough to cut it either."

"No kidding. We used a chisel and hammer. Ha-haa!"

I shook my head and grinned. By this time we were deep into reminiscing, and fishing was a sideshow because the action had slowed. It was good family entertainment.

My fond memories of powdered milk took center stage. "And how about that milk, huh?"

"Oh, I couldn't stand that stuff. It never mixed right. Little puffs balls were always floating around in it."

"And it was tinted yellow for crying out loud. Who drinks yellow milk anyway?" I wondered.

"Plus it was thin, kind of like drinking colored water."

"That milk messed up even the best cereal," I said with disappointment. I was a big cereal eater, and that was a dark time in my cereal eating history.

"At least the farm milk was drinkable," Nub remembered. "But it wasn't fun filling those gallon glass jugs, especially during winter."

Another laugher hit me. "We broke a few of them jugs in the back of the old station wagon. I think in the winter, remember?"

Nub's head popped back. "Yeah. Poor mom. We cleaned it up, but not good enough. Man did it stink when it warmed up!"

"Oh well, it was like Pops said, we always had food on our plates, clothes on our backs, and a roof over our heads."

"We had the basics alright. They made sure of that."

I lifted my worm and gave it another drift, not that I was expecting a fish at that point. Nub was content to let his worm have some peace and quiet on the bottom.

"And speaking of clothes," Nub went on, "I didn't get many new things."

"You! What about me? I wore hand-me-downs for years, and I was the oldest. Explain that!"

While we made fun of our somewhat meager belongings during our youth, we always carried respect for our parents. They both worked hard and provided the necessities. They afforded us a comfortable lifestyle, just not an extravagant one. We understood that, but being who we were, we found humor in ways most people wouldn't.

The more we talked, however, the more we realized that we wouldn't have changed a thing. Our hard-working parents turned us into hard-working people. We valued the dollar and learned to be frugal when we had to. A sense of pride was planted within us as we fought to earn our keep.

Perhaps I was drawn to the Flag because success could only be achieved through hard work. Nobody got freebies on our trips, as our form of "payday" came from grit and determination. Our belongings weren't flashy, but they were functional. A glance at a creel full of trout boasted a sense of accomplishment. We not only worked independently, but we also worked as a unit, which is how we were raised.

Our household and the stream shared many parallels, and I appreciated the character building that I received from both places.

19

Nature's Rake

We finished our round of rehashing and focused back on fishing. Oddly enough, that coincided with an uptick in action as our poles began to dance. The bite was a light tap, but I set the hook anyway.

"I finally got one," I told Nub.

He flashed a look and then locked a beaded stare on his pole. A quick wrist snap properly addressed his twitching rod tip. "Same with me."

"No weight to mine though," I said as the trout splashed on the water's surface. Seconds later, it fell off, thankfully.

"Mine's small too," he said while pulling it in.

"This hole is the biggest let down of the day. I mean, what gives here?" I said, confused and disappointed.

We looked to depart for a fishier place, but the river had other ideas. My feet had sunk into its soft bottom and imprisoned me. I battled against the Flag's gooey grip and eventually wiggled free.

"You ready?" I asked.

"Yeah."

"Let's find another hole. We got to do better than this."

We slogged around the bend and moved towards a strip of sand to exit the water. I stopped so quickly that Nub almost bumped into me.

"What's the deal?"

I grinned and scratched my chin. "Well, I'll be darned. Check it out."

There in the sand among some deer tracks were fresh sets of boot prints. They led away from the hole we had just fished.

"Hmmm. That explains no fish here," Nub said.

"The subordinates got us. They actually listened back there about how to fish a hole," I said with some satisfaction.

"Maybe we taught them too well," Nub joked.

We followed their path to where they had scampered up a slippery clay bank that was gouged with skids marks. A small tree was dislodged and several ferns had been uprooted from their efforts to reach the forest floor—no easy task. Two wily veterans were faced with an ego challenging decision.

"How about we stay in the stream," Nub suggested.

"Good idea. I mean, not that we couldn't get up there, but you know, there might be a good hole up ahead."

"Well yeah, we've scaled banks twice as high and twice as steep!" Nub emphasized.

"Heck, we walked to school every day in a blizzard, going uphill both ways!" I piled on.

We gave that bank a verbal lashing, and then snuck away wanting no piece of it.

We moved forward at a slower pace than earlier in the day. Our bodies felt the effects of several hours on the stream. Now the mosquitoes, they were relentless. Didn't those things ever get tired? They annoyed us more so later in the day, as their energy level stayed the same while ours dropped off.

Nub pulled some backwoods perfume from his vest and sprayed himself, hoping to deter a squadron of biters. It was Chanel No. 2 Muskeeto, I vaguely recall—a scent only an outdoorsman could appreciate. I followed suit, only my bottle was nearly empty.

"You got much left?" I asked.

"Yeah. I bought some new stuff last time."

"Good. I'm about out."

Nub jumped on a business opportunity. "Well, for a mere ten bucks a spray, you can use mine."

"Very funny."

The truth was that stuff was worth its weight in gold on the stream. I suffered through a few experiences to know.

We walked a bit further when a white shore bird jumped up ahead and flew off. That pricked a memory of mine.

"You remember a few years ago when we saw those big crane things on the river?"

"Yeah. I think they were blue herons. They're fish eaters," Nub said distastefully.

"Well, that was unusual. They left tracks everywhere. I hardly remember seeing those things before."

"Yeah, I'm not sure what that was all about. I just know I didn't like them eating our fish."

I liked the sound of "our fish." Of course, we knew they weren't really ours. We just borrowed them from time to time. However, when people get attached to something, they tend to claim it, and indeed we were attached to the Flag.

The river spoke to us in muffled tones while we trudged on a sandy bottom in knee-deep water. With each step, a puff of sediment rose into the water and quickly settled, leaving the current with little to play with.

Up ahead was a kidney-shaped sandbar that nestled inside the river's curve. Water licked our boot bottoms as we trudged up its moist flank. Across from us, the river dug deeply into the earth and formed a long-running ebony trace that rode under the bank like black paint under a ball player's eyes. However, it was the sand-rich bank that captured my attention, for it displayed a beautifully crafted mural. Engraved in its maroon overtone were packages of parallel lines that scrolled across its face. Each package of lines was nearly a foot in length before they terminated into another set at a low angle. The six-foot high, sculpted bank transitioned upward into the forest floor's earthy mat.

The geologist in me won the arm wrestling match over the

fisherman as my worm stayed hooked to the pole. I gazed across the bubbling drink with delight. My brother, as expected, had begun his first drift upstream of me.

"Hey Nub, check out the cross-beds. That's a really nice example of them."

His head popped up and he glanced around.

"Is that another geology thing?" he asked with a hint of annoyance. He went back to fishing before I could answer.

"Well, yeah. I noticed some downstream but I didn't say anything. These are too good to pass up."

Painstakingly, he looked up again. He scanned the far bank. "Is that something over there?" he asked.

"You got it. You see them?"

"Those lines? It looks like somebody took a rake across the bank."

"Or something like that. Those are cross-beds. You're looking at the profile of a point bar, like the one we're standing on."

He snapped his wrist in lightning fast fashion but came up empty. "Dang, I just missed one."

"You oughta pay more attention," I said.

He shook his head with raised eyebrows. I read the sign language. With some guilt, I sent my worm into the dark water for a drift.

"Anyway," I went on, "when geologists see that type of pattern in rocks, we know they were deposited in a river environment."

"What does that matter anyway?" he said while digging in his worm can.

"Once we know the depositional environment, we can better predict the size and geometry of sand bodies. Sand is porous, so fluid travels through it pretty good, even when buried deep in the earth."

"Yeah, and?"

"Well, if there was contamination in the ground, a hydrogeologist could better predict how to clean it up. Or for drinking water, it could help them understand flow through an aquifer."

Nub got it. "Like the water well at my house. I guess that type of thing would help with that."

"Sure. And in the oil business, it helps companies better produce oil and natural gas from sandstone reservoirs down deep."

"Like how deep?"

"Heck, 5,000 to 15,000 feet, sometimes even past 20,000 feet."

I enjoyed visualizing the earth beneath me; it was a necessity in my line of work. What was more pleasing, however, was to explain my thoughts to non-geologists with the earth's features before us. Where I found an open mind willing to learn, I gladly taught.

20

An Extraction

*S*uddenly, my line danced and that ended the geology discussion. There was nothing like knowing a trout was at my doorstep. Even as a veteran fisherman a wave of excitement still washed over me just before setting the hook. The nibbles continued with harder pulls. Timing was everything. Wham! The swimmer hit hard and I welcomed it to my world.

"Feesh-On-Ralphie!" I yelled out. My exuberance bounced off the impenetrable mural and echoed back to us.

The trout ran for a clump of brush on the far bank but I steered it clear of snag danger. It put up a good fight, but in the end, victory was mine. Moments later, I removed the hook from a sleek brook trout and set it free. A push of its tail sent it away with grace.

Nub minded his own business as he hooked a similar version of my trout. It zipped around and sprayed water from its slapping tail, giving us a show.

After the action passed, we fished in silence, and that's when my favorite lullaby made its debut. Daaa, daaa, daa, da-da, daa, da-da. The slow, clear whistling was a distinctive melody that captured the Flag's essence. The beautiful cadence often accompanied my early trips with Gramps and Pops.

Why do simple songs touch humans so deeply? There's something with music that triggers the brain and drops a person's consciousness into another realm. And I felt myself drift away.

Nub yanked some line from his reel and startled me. Another round of the melodic whistling kicked off again.

"Hey, did you hear that?" I asked Nub.

"Huh? Like what do you mean?"

I pulled my line out of the water. "The bird calling. It's the one I heard all the time when I was young, before you got going out here."

We listened together for what seemed like eternity before the bird shared its music with us again. Daaa, daaa, daa, da-da, daa, da-da.

"There! You heard it?" I asked sharply.

"Yeah, it sounds familiar. I didn't pay much attention to it before."

"Well, that's normally background noise for me too," I conceded, "but I've heard it too many times to forget it."

"What's doing it?" Nub wondered.

"I think it's a white-throated sparrow. Of course, I'm no bird watcher. I've never really seen the thing, but the song gives it away."

Nub shook his head in amazement. "You mean you couldn't tell a blue heron but you know about a white-throated sparrow?"

A gentle smile splashed across my face. "I had a little help from a professor at school. I hummed the song and he knew the bird."

I continued drifting in the dark water when my peripheral vision caught a streak of chartreuse that came and went with a plop.

My attention was on Nub's line. "Hey, did you add something to your hook?"

"I put some yarn on. What the heck, huh."

"I suppose. You got nothing to lose out here. I've tried that before but it didn't do much for me."

"Me neither. I'm just trying to shake it up a little bit."

"You're giving that worm a bad hairdo, that's for sure!"

I slid several steps downstream and fished the channel's lower lip. A challenge loomed as two medium-sized poplar trees lay partially submerged in deep water. Their leafless branches splayed everywhere.

"Nubby, I'm going to try this spot."

He passed a look. "Can you get a worm in there?"

I snuck closer to the wooded mess and peered around. "Barely. This is going to be an extraction though. I might need your help."

An extraction was a technical term straight from the Dincau trout fisherman's handbook. The term meant we fished a hole with heavy cover. Sometimes we'd drop our bait in spaces the size of a bread plate, which made it tricky to extract a trout. It didn't always work, but we had success often enough.

My worm dangled over a slot between branches and then did its best impression of Jacque Cousteau. I waited and nothing. I tried another space, and then another adjacent to it. The weak current didn't offer me help in covering ground, so I leaned over for some extended reach fishing, dabbing among brush fingers. Finally, my patience paid off.

"Got one!" I yelled. "Oh man, this is tough."

Nub pulled up and went on high alert. My heart rate kicked up a notch as I wrestled a trout within entangled branches. My pole jiggled and bounced off the tree limbs, making dull clunking noises. The hooked trout was having its way.

The whole experience reminded me of other memorable outdoor adrenaline rushes, like when jetting bluebills buzz your head, or when specklebelly geese delicately descend with feet out and wings cupped, or when the crunching steps of a whitetail buck pierce a silent forest.

The combative fellow fought with grit. I was getting the upper hand when things changed for the worse, as my line caught under a branch. The fish fluttered in response and flashed its sides.

"I'm hung up, Nub," I said while adjusting my feet for better leverage.

"You need some help?"

"Yeah. I can see it down there—a nice one too."

Nub scampered over and waded into thigh-deep water. "It's hung on a branch, but not too bad." He leaned sideways and stuck his leg out. "I'll try to free him with my boot."

He missed the first time, and then steadied himself for another try.

"Hey, you got it!" I said. Instantly, the trout's entire weight was back on my line. "Can you bend a few of those branches down so I can lift him over?"

He dipped his arm in the water. "Give that a try."

I gave a firm, smooth pull. "There we go!" The trout was surgically removed from the brush.

It swam freely into the open stream where it ripped my pole down in violent jerks. I headed towards shore and stumbled sideways, kicking up a plume of dirty water. Nub slowly dislodged himself from his precarious situation and muddied the water even more. I regained my footing and escorted the trout to the sandbank where it slapped its body with disapproval.

"Well Nubby, we got a chunky eleven-and-a-half-inch brown for all our efforts."

"That isn't bad, huh?" he asked.

I contemplated for a second. "I think I'll let it go. I only need one more and we still have more fishing left."

Nub stood alongside me, glanced down his leg and shook some water off his arm. "That's about right. I got water down my boot and a wet shirt sleeve, you know."

"Yeah, that was fun!"

He shook his head and mumbled something. I didn't understand him, fortunately.

"You ready to head out?" I asked.

He looked over the water, which now looked like creamed coffee. "Yeah, this hole is done. We should keep an eye out for the boys."

"Hmmm. Come to think, we haven't seen them in a while. Do you want to walk the bank to make up some ground?"

"I suppose. I don't see any holes ahead anyway."

Nub led the way up a shallow sloped bank that opened into the forest. We weren't long into our jaunt when a large, recently felled pine tree blocked our path. The remnants of a pine cone rested on the tree's broad back, likely the doings of a hungry squirrel. The tree was about four feet off the ground, which made it difficult to go over or under. After we assessed the situation, Nub took the low road and I took the high road, since I was taller. It wasn't easy for either of us. Nub took a shot to the head and was jabbed in the spine by some broken branches. He was reduced to crawling to finally clear it. I was stuck in the ribs by a stiff branch. As I rolled off the log's back end, some bark tore at my neck and gave me a forest hickey. And then an overhanging poplar tree entered the action and grabbed my rod tip. I yanked it free and pulled back a collection of leaves. We each straightened up, albeit rather slowly.

"That wasn't easy," I growled while knocking tree debris off my body.

Nub lifted his hat and held his sore head. "Yeah, that could send a guy into early retirement."

"No kidding. Looks like you lost some more hair."

"Yeah, well, looks like half the forest jumped in your mop."

"Good one," I said while patting him on the back. "That was actually kind of funny . . . for once."

"It's about time you catch up with my humor," he blurted back as we started walking.

Our profiles disappeared into a mob of small pines, although our path could have been traced by the sounds of snapping twigs as we weaved through the natural obstacle course. The pines blended into some alders that held a flushing surprise. We both looked left into heavy cover towards a rush of rapid wing beats.

"Jeez, what was that?" I asked. "It didn't sound big enough to be a grouse."

"Pretty sure it was a woodcock."

"A woodie! I hadn't seen one of those in a while."

A woodcock is a migratory game bird about the size of a dove. It has a distinctive long, pointy beak and a brownish body.

"You know, for all the hunting and fishing we've done, I've only bagged a few woodies," I went on. "Hardly hunted them really."

"Well I have. I've had some great woodcock hunts."

"Really? I guess we haven't talked much about them. We're usually caught up in deer, ducks, grouse or some kind of fishing."

Nub went into story telling mode. "One time I flushed over a dozen of them things. They were flying everywhere and one smacked into my gun barrel. It was rolling on the ground and Coop picked it up."

Cooper was Nub's well-trained springer spaniel. I had my own version of hunting dog in Tango, our beloved black Lab. While we often bragged about their uncanny field and retrieving abilities, the truth was, they were incredible pets and we counted them as part of our families.

I checked the baloney meter on that tale. "So you got a bird without shooting? Are you full of it?"

Nub was a master story embellisher on his own admittance. He had crafted his art for years and developed into a full-fledged professional.

"I'm not making it up. That's the way it happened. It was the weirdest thing."

"Fine. I believe you, but I'm checking with Coop when we get back!"

We commonly mixed hunting stories while fishing and vice versa. Dogs, various animals and all seasons always entered into our discussions. It warmed the innards.

21

A Wizard's Wand

*A*fter we traversed a few more minutes, Nub stepped into an opening and scanned up the stream.

"I see them," he said.

"Good. Finally."

Moments later we looked down upon them from a perch on the bank. They were drifting a noisy set of rapids when we grabbed their attention.

"How she go fellas?" Nub barked with extra volume.

"Good!" they answered in unison.

"I think we almost have our limits," Drew went on. "Mainly all brookies."

"Yeah, we caught a bunch so far," Alex added. "They just keep biting." His tone carried a pitch of excitement.

"We nearly have our limits too. We still have some stream to fish, but let's stay close because we'll hang it up in a while," I said.

It was a bit depressing to mention the end of our trip. My family's vacation to Duluth was drawing to a close. I had a long plane ride back to Louisiana to think about it, so I pushed it out of my mind.

The day's hardships taxed my body, not to mention I wasn't exactly a spring chicken. However, I felt a renewed sense of energy while looking up river. It tapped the explorer in me. Searching the Flag's virgin fingertips carried a sense of discovery. The river became narrower and faster flowing, and although the holes were smaller, they held a special magic because they were untouched by humans.

We departed upstream hurriedly, pulled by the desire to fish new waters in a short timeframe. Once clear of the boys, we took advantage of a low bank and detoured into the river. We dabbled in some poorly defined holes, but still pulled out some beautiful little trout. A break in the action led to some family talk.

"So what's the latest on the girls and their sports?" Nub asked. His tone was casual, which fit our relaxed setting.

"Well, they're still both in soccer, softball, basketball and volleyball."

"Jeez. That's got to be a three ring circus."

"Pretty much. Snez and I are running everywhere," I said, acting out of breath. "I'm still coaching them in soccer and softball, so that makes it even crazier. And don't forget, Alex is in tennis and bowling."

"So he's done with baseball for good then huh?"

"Yeah," I sighed. "He was a good southpaw pitcher, but he hurt his shoulder and then lost interest."

"Speaking of pitching, Drew's been on the mound lately and he's doing a good job." Nub continued on. "So, how old are the girls again?" he asked.

"Amanda is twelve and Nicole is ten," I said while flipping my worm for another drift.

"What do you think they're going to stick with into high school?" Nub's voice faded for a second as he turned to locate a splashing trout downstream.

"I think Nicole likes soccer and basketball best, but they are at the same time in high school, so probably soccer. Amanda is harder to tell. Softball is probably her best sport, so maybe she'll keep going in that." I whisked away a few mosquitoes. "She could do volleyball too because they don't conflict," I went on.

"They're all still doing well in school?"

"Yep. Grades are good and they're hard workers. They know school comes before sports."

I shifted the questions back to Nub. "What about Mandi? I talked to Drew the other day about hockey. He's going a long way in that."

With a pop of enthusiasm, he gave me some details. "Well, first, they're both doing real good in school. It's like you said, school before sports." Nub lifted his worm and sent it to another portion of the hole while he spoke.

"What's she now, like nine or so?" I asked.

"She's eight, but she'll be nine next month. She's doing softball and soccer and I'm coaching the softball stuff."

"Does she like it?"

"Yeah, I think so. Seems like all our kids are into sports, huh?"

"Yep, it runs in the family. Mom and Pops liked it and so do our wives." I paused and went on. "And speaking of, Chris must be on the run with her job and all?"

"Yeah, she stays busy alright. Takes care of the house and all of us among everything else."

Another thought struck me. "You know, the girls tried dance and all three of ours played instruments, but none of it stuck. Now Amanda, she draws once in a while, and real well too. That's from mom's side for sure."

"That's kind of funny. It's the same with us, except I don't think our kids are big into drawing." Nub contemplated for a second. "Must be something in the genes I guess."

I looked around at our wild setting. "You're right. It's something in the genes alright."

"Speaking of genes," Nub added, "maybe the girls would want to come out here?"

"I've mentioned it to them, but they weren't interested yet. Maybe when they get a little older. Now that would be a hoot!"

"I'm all for it. I'm sure Mandi would join them."

Nub expanded our conversation to Mitch. "I think Mitch really likes his girlfriend Kelly. Who knows, maybe he'll finally get married."

"Huh. Maybe they'll have some future trout fishing kids!" I said with a grin.

Our babble was interrupted by snapping branches and thumping feet. The boys cruised by us like we didn't exist. With their heads down, they blasted through the woods hoping to make the most of their last hour.

Nub looked at me incredulously. "Did you see that?"

"Sure did. Those two could have walked into a freight train without knowing it!"

"Couple of subordinates," Nub mumbled.

"How about we head up so they don't get a mile ahead of us?"

"Sounds good. Maybe stay in the stream, huh?"

I pressed my lips in thought. "I suppose. The kids probably walked by some holes."

"You mean ran by," Nub corrected me.

Navigating a rock-filled stream required extra attention. It was like stepping on a pile of slippery softballs. Compounding the problem was a persistent current that pulled at our ankles and tested our balance. At times, we looked half-drunk as we staggered around. Fortunately, we stumbled upon two nice holes after several minutes of wading.

The stream's rapid pulse creased along the left bank and gouged out a deep channel that was underlain with rocks and ribbons of sand. A number of ashen logs and sticks jutted out along the channel's course and made for good trout cover. I moved to the upper hole and drifted the fast water nearest the logs; my worm experienced a bumpy ride down slope.

That type of speedy drift needed a taut line and special attention to keep the sinkers from sagging towards the bottom and wedging between the cobbles. Only a veteran's feel could distinguish between the bumps of a stony bed versus the pull of a trout.

"This looks good, huh Nub?" I said in a low but penetrating voice.

"Yeah. I wonder when the last time somebody fished these spots?"

"It must have been a long time ago . . . because I've got a Feesh-On-Ralphie!" My pole doubled over as the trout took the bait aggressively.

I battled the fish, rocks, and current. The native was relentless, putting both its shoulders into the fight, testing my equipment and my prowess. After a wild ride, I steered it sideways and landed it on a gravel bar. The trout spanked its body on the slick, hard surface. It was a beautiful brookie with a slight hook jaw.

"I have to keep this one Nubby—nothing like a thirteen-incher to round out my limit!"

I slipped him through the square hole in my creel and he flopped around while I covered the hole and dunked the fish and ferns. Water ran out of my wicker container in sieve-like fashion when I straightened up.

Nub glanced towards me before his hands flew up. "Hey, hey!" he shouted. "Feesh-on-Ralphie back at you!"

In short order, Nub deftly worked his trout away from some long reaching sticks and, after a good tussle, banked it.

"Another nice keeper!" he said with enthusiasm. "That's my last one too."

Those trout may have struggled to push a pound, but they were trophies in the narrow virgin waters, fighting like fish twice their size.

We washed our hands with cool river water, added new worm pieces to our hooks and sent out our casts. About halfway through my drift, the line stopped dead in its track and headed slowly back upstream.

"I think I've got another one," I whispered sharply.

Bam! My second trout hit hard and fought with vengeance, perhaps sending me a message for having removed its partner from the stream. The trout darted for cover under a basket of overturned tree roots before I ushered it away into open water. A minute later, I banked it and removed a hook that was stuck in the roof of its mouth.

Nub looked my way. "What you got?"

"An eleven-inch brookie, maybe a hair under," I answered while releasing it. "It's not often I throw back a nice brook trout. What a day!"

"No kidding. It seems like these areas just haven't been fished."

While Nub went back to work, I found myself gazing at Gramps' battle-scarred pole that fit so comfortably in my grasp. I'd lost track of its age, but it was likely my elder. The cork handle was longer than my grip by a few finger widths and was polished to a shine. Its rich bourbon tone was scratched and pockmarked from hooks and rugged use. The pocked crevices had absorbed life from trips gone by and bled starless black. A small square cork was attached with glue and silver duct tape and sat above the handle, serving as the main hook holder for the pole. That was Gramps' homemade addition.

The gold and blue automatic reel was firmly secured below the cork handle at the base of the rod. It was a unique device that operated under the tension of an enclosed spring. Tension increased when line was pulled out and it was released when the lever was pressed to retrieve line. As the spring aged, it became less efficient. To account for that, the blue cap on the reel's face could be turned by hand, which added tension back to the spring.

The pole itself was black and well-balanced. It was stiff enough to handle a lake-run steer, but still sensitive enough to detect the lips of a fingerling. Silver metal eyelets ran the pole's course and were fastened by dark maroon threads that stood the test of time. I had wielded that pole for so many years that it felt like an extension of my hand, imparting the feel of a wizard's wand.

22

Southern Twang

*M*y moments of equipment admiration ended with the sounds of cantaloupe-sized rocks banging into one another. Apparently my partner was drawn to experience some geology for himself.

"Ah hah! You're finally turning into a rock hound," I said with enthusiasm.

Nub knelt at the stream's edge and slowly looked my way, like he was guilty of something. "I'm not looking at rocks, they're just in the way."

"I should have figured." I took a step closer. "Did you drop something?"

"No. I was trying to catch one of those tiny frogs. Thought I'd try it for bait. You know, use the native foods for the trout."

I was intrigued. "So, you got one?"

"Not yet." He straightened his back and worked out a kink. "I'm sure there are some grubs or something under these rocks."

"I'll give you credit for trying, but I'll stay with the worm."

No sooner had I spoke than my line danced softly in my left hand. I waited for the tap-tap-tap to strengthen and then I made my move, but with sour results. My timing was off a smidgen and my hook set came up empty. My worm was still attached with a few bruises.

"Patience, patience," I mumbled to myself.

"Huh?" Nub asked.

"Oh nothing, I just missed one," I told him. "Maybe I'm getting a little tired and losing my edge." I pitched my worm for another drift. "You find anything native to fish with?"

"Nothing big enough."

He put on a new worm piece and looped an underhanded cast into roiled water near some brush.

Out of the blue, Nub fired off an oddball question. "What do you call those drainage rivers down there again? It was a funny name."

I had a confused expression. "You mean like down by my house?"

"Yeah." He bobbled his pole to untangle some line at his rod tip.

My eyebrows pinched together. "Funny? A coulee?"

"Yeah, that's it—coulee. Ha-haa! What a goofy name."

A coulee is a French Canadian name for a drainage valley. Since much of South Louisiana has French roots, it made sense the name was used for the numerous drainage ditches that etched the landscape.

I wasn't sure whether to be offended or break out laughing. "I don't get the funny thing. Why is that so funny?"

Nub held his belly. "Just listen to it. Coouleee."

I shook my head. "That's Louisiana you know. We have all kinds of different names. Remember what they call crappie down there?"

"Ahh, sack of something wasn't it?" he guessed miserably.

"Sac-a-lait," I said. "That was embarrassing."

"Hey, it's lucky I remembered that much!"

"Anyway, they call a bluegill a bream. Plus, there's a speckle trout down there, but it's a saltwater fish with a spike tooth in its mouth." I licked my chops. "Man, they're good eating. My buddy Todd takes me fishing offshore in the summer and we have a heck of a time catching those specks. He's better than any guide, and the funny thing is, it's their family tradition too. Four generations worth just like us!"

"That's cool!" Nub said thoughtfully. "Hey, Gramps sometimes called the brook trout a speck. Remember that?"

"I sure do."

"What about some of those different duck names?" Nub asked.

"Well, your favorite bluebill is sometimes called a dos gris. And they call a ring-neck a blackjack." I sent another cast, but my pole remained lifeless. "They have a local duck down there called a mottled duck. It's big like a mallard but darker and less colorful."

We went silent for a spell, with both of us mentally recalling duck hunts and fishing trips from days gone by. A cool current licked our boots, while thoughts of those outdoor adventures warmed our insides. More time passed; the action had slowed.

Our telepathy was evident as we pulled our worms from the drink and secured our hooks. We traded glances and turned side by side to navigate a flowing sheet of lumpy dark water that looked to be hammered from a cast iron pan. Rocks of all sizes reared up from the river and arched their backs, while their submerged brethren rested below with slippery faces. The river's untamed edges rode roughshod down slope and blew everything wild into my nostrils. Life was fresh and freewheeling.

The August day's heat reached its high of eighty degrees, and a trickle of sweat down my temple reminded me of it. Between careful steps, I lifted my ball cap and gave my head a breather.

Up ahead, the stream slanted to the right, but before doing so, a relatively large tributary flowed into the Flag from the left side. A number of small, spring-fed tributaries flowed into the Flag, so it wasn't an uncommon site. This one, however, was nearly big enough to fish.

"Didn't you fish this once?" I asked.

"Yep. I even caught one back in there."

"A ten-incher, right?"

"Well, maybe a twelve-incher."

I cast a wary eye towards him. "I'm going to have to start taking pictures."

"Hey, I'm rounding up—fisherman's math you know! Anyway, there's one bigger hole back in there. Kind of surprising since the thing is only five feet wide or so."

I jabbed Nub in the arm. "Well, you going to give her a try?"

He paused and adjusted his cap. "Nah, not today. The water looks a little low."

The main river carried noticeably less water than it had at the bridge, which was due to being upstream of several tributaries and a number of tiny springs. Those small creeks and springs added important water volume to the main river, and we noticed the effects of their contribution more so now.

"How far up you think the kids are?" Nub asked while he jostled for footing.

"Not sure, but let's keep going until we see them. As Pops would say, let's hoof it."

Nub spilled a light laugh.

"You remember that?" I asked.

"Yeah, Pops and his sayings…"

"Let's hit the woods, that'll be faster," I suggested.

"Sounds good."

I looked up the river as a last check for the kids, but instead I only saw a tumbling waterway with thick foliage shingling its periphery.

Fortunately, the stream was smaller and the banks lower versus downstream, which made leaving the stream easier. We traipsed our way through an array of forest entanglements and stopped to fish a few small holes. Minor success with the trout kept us moving.

I was leading the way when Nub slowed and noticed a jug-sized brown object that resembled a bundle of parchment paper.

"What are you looking at?" I asked while slightly out of breath.

He pointed low towards a clump of alder branches. "Looks like an old wasp's nest."

"Maybe there's still something in it."

"Nah, it looks dead. Not like the one you banged into that one time and sent wasps all over me," he scowled.

"Oh yeah, I forgot about that!"

"I suppose, I'm the one who got bit," he sharply reminded me.

"And to this day your head and face are still puffed up," I joked.

"Fine, I'll take the lead and you can get stung if we run into anything." He bolted past me with a few powerful strides and we continued our search, only at a faster clip.

Several minutes later we spotted the young fishermen standing on a spread of gravel in ankle-deep water. They were having quite a time, laughing and throwing their bodies back. We ambled down the bank and splashed across scalloped water.

"What the heck's going on here? Are you two having a party by yourselves?" I asked in a light tone.

They straightened up momentarily.

"Well, Drew stepped in a mushy spot over there and went over his boot. He got all wet," Alex laughed.

Drew attempted to lessen the jab. "Yeah, but my boot was leaking anyway, so it didn't matter much."

Alex was relentless. "You're wet up to your butt now though."

"What about you?" Drew fired back. "You slipped on a rock and got water in both your boots!" he said with a giggle.

Nub and I shook our heads. "What a couple of subordinates, huh, Nub?" I asked with sliver of humor.

"Just what I was thinking," he replied. "It's amazing they made it this far!"

Of course, we were kidding. The boys handled the rugged terrain admirably and caught a lot of fish on their own. We were really quite proud of them, but they needed their wings clipped occasionally.

"Are you guys finished here?" Nub asked, although the answer was obvious. They nodded yes.

There wasn't a trout in its right mind that would have hung around after their ruckus.

"Nubby, you want to grab my water from my back pocket for me?" I asked.

He stepped over and helped me out, and then I returned the favor. We each took a few swallows and then crunched up our empty plastic bottles so they took less space. We needed to rehydrate before our impending long walk back to the truck.

"You boys have any water left?" Nub asked.

"Nah," they replied.

Alex looked a bit distraught. "I had almost a half-bottle before I shared it with Drew because he was out."

Drew squinted and listened close.

"Anyway, he drank about the whole thing. So I got nothing left."

"Ahh, come on Alex, I took one sip," Drew said, defending himself.

"Oh right, you took about three or four big gulps!" Alex hammered back.

Nub stepped in to ease the mild bickering. "Jeez anyway, that's enough you two. Leave some for the end," Nub instructed. "You never know what might happen out here."

I looked at the boys. "You guys ready to head upstream?"

"Yeah," they responded in unison as they gave each other a playful shove.

"Let's stay together," I suggested. "We'll try a few more holes and then call it quits."

The boys frowned in discontent. Nobody likes to acknowledge a trip's final hour.

23

Reflections

*F*our fishermen on a narrow stream wasn't an optimal situation, so we let the boys take the lion's share of the fishing. Nub and I sauntered along while the kids pulled out some colorful brookies that would have made a seasoned angler salivate. We released them all, however, as greed didn't have a placemat at the Flag. Also, we wanted to teach our kids respect for the law by adhering to the limit. We've only had a few run-ins with game wardens over the years, and they were without incident.

The final chapter of our fishing day was melancholy for me. It was a feeling I'd grown used to over the years, especially since I'd moved down South, which limited my Flag fishing trips.

My energy level dropped off as I sensed the next hole was our last. The weight of the day's physical strain came down hard upon me. I looked upstream and had the urge to keep going, to keep exploring, but we had gone far enough. Logic had finally overcome emotion. We had a long walk back, and the thought of adding more distance wasn't appealing.

The boys were fishing a narrow hole and Nub was nearby putting the finishing touches on a small trout. I slugged ahead and eyed a small bowl of water snuggled against the left bank. It had the potential to hold a few trout. Just above that area, a gravel bar with sand patches sprawled out and dipped its flanks into the shallows. A few large logs and rocks were strewn about by nature's chance. It was a great place to stop and clean trout.

In the meantime, I had a hole to fish. It wasn't big, but it looked deep and inviting. A small waterfall plunged off a cluster of roots and dug into the stream's bed. The water swirled and frothed while it righted itself from the drop. Regaining momentum after the plunge, the flow crawled from its hollow and spilled freely back into the river's mix.

My drooping profile flanked the hole, while a knee-deep current leaned against my leg like a tired Labrador. I dropped my worm straight down since there wasn't an upstream drift option. Immediately a trout introduced itself, with my pole bending to its weight. I really wanted to savor the bite, but then again, I didn't want a swallowed hook, so I answered with a sharp lift.

"Feesh-On-Ralphie!" I yelled downstream. "Yeah, baby!"

My rod tip hammered at the water's surface as I played out the fish. I took my time and enjoyed the moment, pulling in the scene like I was out of body and looking down upon myself. A minute later I landed its flopping body on some slick gravel where it delivered more face slaps than the *Three Stooges*.

"A nine-inch brookie," I hollered to my partners. "They're still biting!"

They gave me a look, but didn't say anything. Maybe the day was wearing on them too.

I tried the little pocket of erupting water again, but only got a few small nibbles. It was a one trout hole, which didn't surprise me. I stared into the drink with pole in hand and watched bubbles of oxygen continuously rise to the surface. It was a beautiful show, kind of like a lava lamp, only with relaxing sounds.

For all practical purposes, I was done fishing. I sent my worm to different edges of the hole, knowing the results would be fruitless. It didn't matter. What really mattered was that I was here, still part of the stream.

A trout fisherman knows when he's struck an accord with the river, as it no longer flows around him, but flows through him instead. The river's pulse becomes absorbed by the angler, and the two eventually act in tandem like a horse and rider. Like my grandfather, I had fallen victim to nature's caress. I had developed a deep affection for this river, much like how a hunter gets attached to his loyal dog.

The river itself was simple in many ways, yet still wonderfully complex. I hadn't unraveled all of the stream's secrets, but then again, I didn't want to. It was part of the lure, part of the mystique. I only hoped to grow old with it like my family before me.

The harmony I'd achieved here brought much happiness and peace. It struck me that those virtues are what families strive to have with each other. Perhaps I was drawn here because it offered a harmony that I could take back to my daily life.

Our trips were tough but forgiving, challenging but achievable, and hopeful amid sprinkles of disappointment. We were encouraged to explore and learn through hard work and patience. Our efforts required ambition and personal accountability shrouded in a veil of respect for the environment. The river's wild surroundings humbled us, and yet it accepted us as we were. Wouldn't I become an outstanding man if I could act and teach in the same regard?

"What do you think?" Nub called up to me, breaking my meditations.

I was slow to answer. As he approached, I finally replied, "I think we're done." My solemn expression answered his question more loudly than words. "Maybe tell the boys to wrap it up so we can clean our fish."

"Yeah. We've been out here quite a while."

I walked to the gravel bar and propped my pole against the bank, while behind me, the sounds of sloshing boots blended with the river's rush. I removed my belt and worm can because it was uncomfortable to sit and bend over with a can on the hip.

Amid the shallow waters was a large rock shaped like a hippo's head—a perfect seat. I sat on its dark snout and placed my creel on the downstream side of the rock, with the sheltered splash acting as a cooler.

Above me, the lower half of a bare-skinned tree lunged over the stream. Around me, rocks of all sizes were scattered about; the smaller ones were crowned with mossy green coats. Their larger kin were bald-topped, but their sides held fast to threads of fleshy algae that wavered in the current.

I had begun cleaning my fish, when Nub and the boys tromped across the gravel bar and shed some of their equipment.

"How's it looking?" Nub asked as he peered in my direction.

"Good. What a limit!" I said while hoisting my largest trout in the air.

Cleaning stream trout was easy. A cut up the belly and one across the base of the gills allowed the angler to pull the innards and clean the blood along the spine. The gills themselves were the last to go. I had finished cleaning a few when I checked on my partners.

"Alex and Drew, you two remember how to clean trout?"

"Yeah, it's not that hard," they responded while reaching into their creels.

Nub swung by and examined their technique, and then continued on to a fallen log where he claimed his perch at the stream's edge.

All four of us had our heads down with busy hands. I raised my eyes and stole a glance at the group, catching a meaningful scene.

"Go easy around the spine so you don't pop the bones away from the meat," Nub reminded the boys.

"Yeah, I had a little problem with the first one," Alex admitted.

I slipped my last cleaned trout back into the creel, and stared into a spread of water. A faint reflection cast an image of a trout fisherman that bore resemblance to me, or was it my grandfather, father, or my son? The wavy image melded a family tree of fishermen and gave me a warm feeling.

"Hey, look at this," Drew piped up. He held up an elongated mass of orange eggs. "This is spawn, right?"

"You betcha! I had one like that," I said.

"Well, they are fall spawners," Nub added. "And the browns too."

Drew flung the lumpy mass into the stream where it was gobbled up by a hungry current. With some remorse, I wondered how many future trout just went floating away.

"Don't trout eat that stuff?" Alex asked.

"Yeah," Nub quickly answered. "We've tried it a few times here, but worms work better."

"The steelhead fishermen use it a lot though, eh Nub?" I asked.

"That's one of the things they use."

I got up, one-handed my creel from the water and splashed over to the boys. They each were on one knee cleaning trout at the stream's edge. They set their cleaned trout on the ground for display, so I stooped over for a closer look and added some to the group.

"What a catch, huh guys?" I asked Drew and Alex.

They gave a half-interested nod and continued with their task. I grabbed the two wicker creels and a worm can and set them by the fish. It was a picturesque scene, with tufts of long grass and several gallon-sized rocks flanking the trout, which lay on a gravel platter.

A Bountiful Harvest

"Hey, Ralphie," I called to Nub. "Look at this set up. Kind of like those pictures in *Outdoor Life,* don't you think?"

He had just finished his last fish so he eagerly came over. "Yeah, that's nice. Shows our great day in a nutshell." He popped up his brim.

"It's too bad their colors fade," Nub said as he pointed to one particularly drab fish.

"Yeah, they look their best when they're first caught. Look at this one; it absorbed the pattern of a fern in this one spot." I lifted the trout and examined its back end.

Nub looked closely at it. "Sometimes that happens when they're in the creel for hours."

We picked up our stuff and checked on the boys.

"When you guys are done, remember to take your knives," I reminded them.

Nub and I went back for our poles, held them out in front of us like we were shooting a gun, and pulled them apart. We dug in our vest pockets and found two twist ties each, which we used to bind the two rod pieces together. It was much easier walking through the woods with a shortened pole.

The boys, on the other hand, were struggling with their pole-separating technique.

"What's going on over there?" Nub asked. "Are you guys wrestling with your poles?"

"Or maybe dancing with them?" I said with a chuckle.

"They're stuck," they replied through clenched teeth.

"That's where the nose oil trick comes into play," I reminded them.

"We did that," they replied.

Nub stepped closer to them. "Look, it won't pull apart with it straight up and down." He took Drew's pole and held it parallel to the ground. "Try it like this."

After a few attempts, they each got it.

While they dealt with their gear, I pushed my finger around inside my worm can. "Nub, you need worms for anything?"

"Nah. I have to work all week, and we have kid stuff next weekend. Just toss them."

We repaid the trout population for a great day by emptying our worm cans into the stream. That was our thank you.

24

A Vest for Life

*W*e lingered for a bit, mainly because we weren't looking forward to a long walk. Out there we measured distance in time, knowing five hours or so of fishing, lunching, and lounging resulted in about forty-five minutes of downstream hiking. In reality, we covered almost a mile as the crow flies, but that didn't count for much, especially since the river's course did figure eights along a straight line.

I took one last look around and saturated my senses. With my cup filled, I lowered my cap brim and led the group into the woods.

Our scramble through the forest resembled the Flag River's version of an NFL Scouting Combine. We high-stepped over stumps, spun around looming hardwoods, busted through sweeping pine branches, and plowed over saplings. Sometimes we carried our creels like footballs, protecting them from nature's relentless grasp.

Fifteen minutes later we felt the heat of late afternoon as streaks of sweat slid down our temples. Although we were shaded during most of our jaunt, our body temperatures rose from the exercise. We missed the cooling effects of the water.

"Ready to try the stream for a bit?" I asked Nub, who was freeing his rod end from a pine bough.

While he tussled, I pulled out some aspen leaves that were wedged between my handle and reel.

"Yeah, let's give it a try." He leaned over and peered downstream. "Careful on the rocks."

One by one we stumbled down the bank and plopped into the water. We navigated the stream slowly at first and then sped up as we gained confidence in our steps, which led to trouble.

"Whoa," I shouted while losing my balance, looking like a giraffe on ice skates. "Watch out for this rock; it's slippery as heck. There's some kind of slime on it."

We stopped as I regained my footing.

"You alright?" Nub asked.

"Yeah, I'll make it. Caught a gulp of water in my boot though." The boys snickered in the background, which I caught wind of. "Watch it, kids—your turn might be next."

It was one thing to walk a rocky stream, but entirely another to walk it downstream, hampered by cloudy water. It was like walking blindfolded at times.

Up ahead the stream deepened and was choked with fallen timber, so we found the woods again and continued our trek without exchanging words. We challenged ourselves to get back efficiently, which required skill in reading the terrain. The trick was to "cut out" the river's curves and walk the easiest, straightest path back to the truck, which put us in and out of the stream.

"Hey, Uncle Tony, hold up for a second," Drew called.

"What's the matter?" I stopped and turned.

Nub's hand was over his eye, Drew had his cap knocked off, and Alex had a painful expression while he shook his hand. Talk about the walking wounded.

"You alright?" I asked Nub.

"Yeah, I think so. I took a twig to the eye." He dropped his hand and stood there blinking. "I'll be alright."

I looked past Nub towards the boys. "You guys okay?" I asked.

"Yeah," Drew answered, "a branch knocked my cap off."

"A wasp or something stung my finger back there," Alex explained.

"That's nice, real nice. Are you going to make it?" I asked Alex.

"Yeah. It kind of hurts though."

"See!" Nub said. "The last guy in line gets hammered by a wasp again."

We resumed our route and plodded through the woods in caravan style, keeping a strong pace when possible.

Suddenly, I stopped on a dime. "What do you think, jump it?" I asked.

A six-foot deep, dry tributary channel impeded our path forward. Its narrow width made it tempting to jump over.

Nub checked it out. "Nah, a little too wide. Plus, it's got a good drop."

I agreed, and one by one we slid down the bank, but before climbing the other side, something caught my eye.

"Hey, look at that thing," I said while pointing to a wet area on the channel bottom.

A circular clay spot the size of a serving plate oozed water from its center.

"I betcha that's a natural spring," I told everyone.

Nub snooped in. "Looks like it. I wouldn't step in that thing. Probably sink in over your boot."

That thought set us back in motion, so up the brick-red bank we went, using tree roots and branches to reach level ground, while protecting our reels from the earth's smudges.

Onward we traveled, through the woods and in and out of the stream. Occasionally we caught a glimpse of a hole we'd already fished, which tempted us to dip a line, but we stayed the course instead. Sandbars riddled with footprints reminded us of our previous efforts.

After forty-five minutes of walking, I spotted a welcome sight.

"Hey, there's the bridge up ahead!" I announced to the group. "Whew, that's a sight for sore eyes."

A blast of adrenaline carried us the last fifty yards through the woods, until finally, our feet rested on the metal bridge. I borrowed a spot on its rusted rails and rested my arms, thoughtfully staring upstream. My pulse was a bit high after our jaunt, but my blood pressure was low from the day's therapy. The Flag itself looked strangely weary, as if pumping water all day to Lake Superior and dealing with our doings took its toll.

The boys shifted around and then worked their way towards the truck. Nub slipped on his sunglasses, joining me in an upstream gaze. The sun shrouded us, its light reflecting off the forest dust that speckled our sweaty arms. Our hands and elbows were clay-stained with nature's version of red shoe polish.

And then, as if on cue, a white-throat's parting hymn sifted down the Flag's watery ribbon and lost itself around us. The wilderness tune brought to life everything the Flag River Valley had offered us that August day.

We stood motionless and peaceful. We were proud, yet humbled. We were beaten, yet victorious.

"Well, the end of another trip," I nonchalantly mentioned to Nub.

"Another one in the books," he replied. "As Gramps and Pops would say, it was an outing."

"Yeah, another one of their sayings," I said lightly, lowering my head in recollection.

"How many you think we caught?" Nub asked.

My head popped back up. "Maybe 100?"

"At least that!" he replied in almost hurtful fashion. "Maybe closer to 150."

"That's thirty to forty each—it could be," I thought out loud.

"Well, actually, thinking about it that way, maybe we got closer to 200," Nub let on.

The bubbling pot of fishermen's stories was on high flame at that point.

"How about we call it 250 for a nice round number?" I was greasing the wheels. "One thing's for sure, this trip is one of the best ever."

We may have caught 500 trout by conversations end, and wrestled a bear and tamed a mountain lion during our adventure, if we hadn't been interrupted.

Doink. Doink. Sharp sounds of rock against metal pierced the air.

"The kids are at it again, eh, Nub," I said with a grimace.

Doink.

"I suppose we should get to the truck. It sounds like they're getting better at hitting that sign."

I looked in their direction. "Or maybe they're just standing closer to it."

"Ha. Look at that! They're almost on top of it," Nub noticed.

We slugged our way over to them. "Come on guys, let's get going," I said.

"Hey, even I could hit that thing from there," Nub heckled the boys.

"We're kind of tired," they replied.

We dropped the tailgate and gathered around the truck. I felt a bit dazed, almost numb, but in a good way. Our great adventure worked its magic on me because I literally lost my place in everyday life during the escapade. Now that's the earmark of a fine trip!

The cooler lid cracked open. "You want a horn, Ralphie?" Nub asked me in traditional style.

A dripping wet, glacier-cold beer appeared in my hand before I could answer. My dry throat welcomed an avalanche of frothy liquid.

"Wow, is that good!" I said while wiping my mouth.

That was one of my best beers ever and it had nothing to do with the label.

The kids gulped their sodas and Nub made his beer disappear in a few swigs. After our thirsts were satisfied, we started stripping off our gear. Sploosh!

"Jeez, Drew," Nub said.

Drew looked up as he finished removing his first hip boot.

"Is that from going over your boot?" Nub asked.

"Nah, my feet were wet all day. I told you these boots leaked."

Another splash followed as he removed his second boot.

"Hey Drew, any trout swimming in there?" I asked and laughed.

Alex was quiet as he tussled with his own boots. Splash! Another gush of water hit the ground.

"Looks like we need to fix some leaks," Nub stated.

"Yeah, I think we have a few patches. We can try dad's old rubber stick, or what's left of it."

"A rubber stick?" Alex asked.

"Gramps and Pops used to heat the end of the rubber stick and rub it over the leaky area," I told them. "It worked. They carried that thing in their vest all the time for quick repairs."

Moments later, several pairs of wet socks were strewn in the truck bed. Mine were included in the count, and even though they didn't get a river soaking, they were damp from sweat. The dry air felt great on our feet.

We transferred our precious cargo from the creels to a couple of gallon-sized freezer bags and then iced them. The moist ferns that lined the creels had done their job admirably, but it was time for us to part ways, so we flung them to the ground.

We slammed the tailgate on our packed gear, with Gramps' old fishing vest topping the heap. Its off-white color and tight weave boasted stains from several decades of trips. The blemishes were a concoction of fish slime, worm juice, mosquito spray, and guts from the Flag River itself. A dark brown leather strip ran from shoulder to shoulder and gave it a handsome look. All the pocket snap buttons still worked, which was a testament to the vest's craftsmanship. It rode high on my torso due to my long frame, but it was still functional. It was indeed a vest for life.

25

River Poker

We all piled into the truck, chased by hungry mosquitoes. Unfortunately, a blast of oven-baked air forced us to roll down the windows for survival.

"Let's get rolling," I demanded while slapping at some mosquitoes.

"It's hot back here," the kids complained.

Nub cranked up the Ford and we exited down the narrow gravel road, picking our way around a string of potholes. A row of tall canopy cast a late afternoon shadow over the country lane, concealing to some degree the road's imperfections. We had a four-hundred-yard drive before the road hooked right at the Fork's gravel parking lot.

"I always liked this stretch of road," I told Nub. "Doesn't it remind you of the old tote roads we've grouse hunted?"

"Yeah, it's got that look alright. You see that cover on the edges, they like that stuff. And they have some gravel to peck at."

I leaned out the window to catch a breeze and get a clean look up the road.

"Why do grouse like gravel again?" Alex asked.

Nubby jumped all over that question. "Well, they have a second stomach called a gizzard. The grit and gravel goes in there and helps grind up their food." Nub paused and grinned. "It's kind of like your dad, Alex. He's got to have a second stomach for how much he eats."

I pulled my head back in. "Yeah, yeah. Very funny. Hey, speaking of eating, remember the spoiled milk incident when we camped at the Forks?" I asked.

Nub's face tightened with a sour expression. "Oh, yeah. I had a bowl of cereal in the morning and about threw up." His body quivered in disgust. "The milk went bad, but I didn't figure it out until after a few big scoops."

The kids got a charge out of that mishap.

"Hey, let's go through the parking lot before heading out," I suggested, since it was just ahead. "We'll show you kids where we camped a few times on our overnight trips."

"You guys camped at the Forks?" the kids asked.

"Oh yeah," I replied. "It made sense since we fished both forks."

"Nice and quiet too," Nub added. "Nobody bothered us."

As it turned out, our plan for a brief parking lot visit experienced a twist in the form of unexpected company.

"Hey, somebody's here," the kids pointed.

Our eyes swept across the square opening, but we didn't notice the parked truck until it was too late. A couple of old fishermen pulled gear from their truck bed and looked up, a bit surprised. They shadowed their eyes and squinted in our direction.

"Just keep going in," I said to Nub. "We can turn around and head out."

"Well, how about that? We finally ran into some old timers that chair fish at the Forks," Nub said in amusement.

"One of those old timers might be you one day," I lightly reminded him.

We had started to leave when one of the fishermen began walking in our direction, albeit rather slowly.

"Looks like this fella wants to talk," I said while rolling down my window.

"Watch what you say," Nub instructed as he stepped on the brake.

Talking to another fisherman while on the same stream is a tricky situation. The approach mimics a gunfight, where each person sizes up the other. The interaction is similar to a poker game, where players try to gain information without showing their hand. The stakes can be huge, especially at the Flag.

A pleasant-faced elderly man in worn denim approached us with measured steps; his beat-up sneakers shuffled in the dirt, and a fisherman's cap covered sprouts of grey hair. He had the relaxed look of someone who'd been on vacation for twenty years.

Behind him, his plump partner leaned on their truck's tailgate and wrestled with a pair of knee-high rubber boots. He threw us a patient glance, revealing thin patches of white whiskers that glistened in the sun. His cheeks hung low like a pair of used saddlebags.

I spoke first as his more agile partner pulled up to my window. "Howdy! How's it going today?"

"Just fine, thank you. Just fine indeed."

A genuine tone matched his trusting face. His overhanging brim shaded a pair of bushy eyebrows that had grown together like an unkempt mustache, their white bristles reaching high towards the crags in his forehead. But it was his mellow eyes that caught me off guard. They drifted in like the river's current, holding tales of a thousand fishing trips. I had seen that look before, a long time ago.

"Are you two just coming in?" I asked.

"Yeah, we just got here." He moved his cap a touch higher on his head. "Figured we'd give the Forks a try. Did you guys fish there already?"

"No, it's all yours. We tried above the bridge on the left fork."

"How'd you do?"

I knew that was coming. "Not too bad. You know, we threw back a lot of little ones, but it was still action."

"Any big browns?" he asked.

"Nah, mainly brookies. Years ago we caught lots of browns and rainbows downstream of here. But those days are over."

"I remember those times," he said with a solemn stare.

"So, how many years have you been fishing here?" I asked.

"Oh, Lord knows. A long time off and on."

"Did you know Ido or Ray Dincau?" I asked with a hopeful expression.

His jaw hinged forward. "Nah, that doesn't sound familiar."

"Ido was my grandfather and Ray is my father. They started me out here thirty-five years ago." I turned and pointed to my partners. "This is my brother and our boys. That's the fourth generation of trout fishermen in the back seat. We're sort of passing the torch," I said proudly.

"Well, I'll be darned," he said. The veteran angler nodded and smiled. "That's something they'll always hold on to."

"How about you, any family fishermen?" I asked.

"No, not really. That's a friend of mine back there." He thumbed behind him. "You got something special here—keep it going," he said sincerely.

"Don't worry about that. We'll keep our tradition alive."

"Well, I just wanted to say hi," the old man said. "I suppose we should get fishing." He stepped back from the truck in slow motion, indicating his intentions.

"Hey, nice meeting you," I said. "And good luck fishing!" We sent them off with a casual wave.

Slow-rising dust clouds followed us as we left the anglers behind. Our truck crawled ahead, plucking pieces of gravel from the road's face and spitting them sideways. Our moderate speed agreed with me. We had three miles of dirt road ahead of us before hitting Highway 13, and I relished that travel time to reminisce.

The kids mumbled amongst themselves, and Drew finally spoke up. "Uncle Tony, why did you tell that guy that we didn't catch much? I mean, we have our limits!"

It was time to teach trout fishing 101 on information sharing. "I told him we caught a lot of little ones. Which was true, right?"

"Well, yeah, but we caught bigger ones too."

"We sure did. But he didn't need to know that. He didn't ask that specific question, so I kept quiet."

Alex joined his cousin in a tag team of questions. "But dad, you told him we didn't catch any big browns. I caught one that's in the cooler."

"Big is a relative term. I think he meant big in like several pounds, like the ones that leave the lake to spawn up here." I turned to make eye contact with the boys. "You get what I'm saying? I was truthful, but I didn't show my hand."

"Yeah, I guess," they replied.

"If you want to keep things a secret, you have to be secretive," I said, driving the point home.

One mile later, the Flag River wiggled out of the woods and snuggled against the road like a Cheshire Cat. Our beloved road stretch greeted us on our way out.

"Hey Nub, how about slowing down up here?"

Under Nub's guidance, the truck drifted left. We sat high in our seats and viewed the river below.

"See, over there, that's where Gramps caught six trout under some logs back when I was a kid." I pointed to a partially shaded area of the stream. "It looked a lot different back then."

"How about our family trips here?" Nub reminded me. "Remember Pops and Mom took us all to the Flag a few times?"

"Oh yeah, that was really something," I said, shaking my head.

"Mitch might have been, what, five maybe?" Nub laughed as he spoke. "It was a small miracle nobody drowned."

Our family trips rivaled the Barnum and Bailey Circus, complete with shrieks of laughter, loads of surprises, and gasps of fright. Three energetic boys scooted around with fishing poles in hand, fueled by a gurgling river loaded with trout. Well, at least in our minds it was. A fairly steep bank connected the road to the river, which made things interesting.

I doubt all three of us boys actually fished at the same time, between the snags, lost bait, being thirsty, a hook in the pants, line entanglements, a spontaneous wrestling match, and a multitude of other distractions. Add some hungry mosquitoes, a mother who didn't like worms, and a father thin on patience, and the recipe for family "fun" was complete.

As we've grown older, we reflect on those days not only with humor, but also with admiration and respect for our parents. Those trips were riddled with imperfections, but our way of family time in a natural setting branded us for life, making a lasting impression. Our hovering over the same fishing hole thirty years later was proof enough.

"Did you guys ever catch any fish?" the boys asked.

Nub and I traded glances.

"Well, we caught a few," Nub blurted out.

"Mainly rainbows, huh, Nub?" I added.

"Yeah, we got a few keepers too, I think."

The boys filtered through our tentative talk. "So, you didn't catch much," they reasoned.

Nub elected to step on the gas and move on, which was fine with me.

"Hey, we were little, and we only fished in that one spot off the road. We didn't have any hip boots or anything like you guys," I reasoned with the kids.

They continued launching their assault. "So, basically you stank at fishing when you were like us?"

"Hey, wait a minute, we were younger than you and we still caught some," I defended.

"You guys didn't know what you were doing, just admit it," they pressed on.

"Oh, jeez. You two are like pesky mosquitoes," I said and waved them off.

The boys were getting a little too big for their britches.

26

Hairpin Highlights

*S*hortly afterwards we crossed back over the first bridge, which put the river on our right. From this point the Lower Flag wandered a quarter mile from the road before nearly rejoining it by the gravel pit, which was a mile's drive downstream from the bridge. That stretch of stream was chockfull of memories for me.

I looked Nub's way. "We have lots of history through this lower stretch, huh?"

"Oh yeah." He was all in for the talk, so he fired off first. "There's that rundown little cabin we camped by a few times." He tossed a shot of snoose in his cup.

We scanned the right side wood line. Off in the distance, guarded by a brigade of mature cedars, was a saggy outline that barely resembled a structure. An overgrown road led in its direction.

"That was a while ago," I said. "I doubt we could get back there now."

"What a great place to camp though. We were next to the stream and under all those cedars," Nub said, briefly lost in thought.

"We fished right from our campsite! Now that was cool," I added.

A few blocks later my hand broad brushed through an open window. "Somewhere back in those woods is The Logjam fellas," I said in a voice loud enough to overcome the road noise.

"Is it still any good?" the boys asked.

"I'm not sure. We haven't been back there in a while. We're probably due for another try, eh Nub?"

"Yep, maybe on our next trip."

The Logjam was an impossible combination of wooden debris that had existed since I started fishing. The mountain of material contained a variety of trout holes. The challenge was pulling them out without falling in ourselves. Sometimes we dinked and dunked in openings no bigger than a shoe box, but that added to the allure.

I still remember having dissected that hotspot with my father on several occasions, and one time in particular, back when lamb chop sideburns were all the rage. There stood Pops, high on the heap's crest, with his hands working the line and his rod tip buried in an opening that sprung from the miserly grasp of the giant set of matchsticks.

He towered above me with a clouded sky as his backdrop, and stood with knees bent as if on center stage. And rightfully so, as his looks were a rare combination of Elvis Presley and Roy Orbison, complete with dark features, black horn rimmed glasses, and a wide jaw line. However, it's likely those stars never donned a ball cap, fishing vest, and hip boots when they performed.

Pops put on a show worthy of admission. While I landed a scrappy trout on the pile's edge, Pops' thumping pole arced under the weight of a large fish. Moments later, a forearm-long brown emerged from the jumbled mass, its smooth, muscular body flexing in mid-air. Pops stepped back and trapped it against his body, later lifting his trophy with an extended arm.

"Feesh-On-Ralphie!" he yelled, his triumphant call overcoming the river's shout.

We caught a half-dozen more trout at The Logjam that day, but none compared to the beauty of Pops' big brown, for which I had the best seat in the house.

That was one of many fine trips with Pops. He was a veteran on the Flag, however, he didn't start there until he was in his mid-twenties, back in the early 1960s. While growing up, he fished in other places with friends, just not the Flag. Since Gramps didn't start fishing the Flag until the mid-1950s, it was tough for a young Pops to get a foothold on our family's prized stream, especially since Gramps had a tight group of friends that he ventured with. Also, Pops had a two-year stint in Army training in Missouri after high school, but later settled back in Duluth. He then worked at a cement plant with an erratic schedule that changed every two weeks, which cut into his ability to make family fishing trips. However, after he married and his work schedule stabilized, he started frequenting the Flag with Gramps. In later years, those trips blossomed into family adventures involving my brothers and me. Sometimes mom even climbed aboard. Pop's had his own style, his own flair, and he made our trips fun. By his mid-forties his interest for trout fishing had waned with his near vision and he called it quits, but not before passing our ways to his sons, especially to me, the eldest.

The Flag was a family bonding place, even back when Pops was a young man. It was a peaceful refuge that we enjoyed in the form of day trips and overnight camping trips. That type of setting fit our family's pistol for four generations.

"I had some great trips with Pops back there, but did you know that I fished with a girlfriend on this stretch?" I asked.

"Yeah, I think you mentioned it once before," Nub foggily recalled.

"She probably out-fished you!" the kids joked in the back.

"Well, we caught a lot of trout that day. I caught most of them because she was just learning. I think we only brought one pole to keep things simple." I paused in thought for accurate recall. "Turns out, we finished up just before The Logjam."

"Any nice ones?" the kids asked while they slurped on their sodas.

"A bunch. Some real nice browns and a few chunky rainbows." I removed my hat and gave my head a breather. "Anyway, at the end of our trip I gave her the pole while I cleaned the trout. I had flipped the worm in the middle of the stream so it wouldn't get snagged up. It seemed like a "safe" place for her to fish. A minute later, she said something was pulling on her line. Of course, I was a little ticked because I assumed she was hung up."

"This stream is tough on amateurs," Nub commented.

"She was hung up alright," I said. "Hung up on a huge brown!"

Nub's eyebrows lifted and the kids leaned forward as if the trophy apparition appeared before them.

"I couldn't believe it myself. She was whooping and hollering."

"She got it in by herself?" Nub asked.

"Pretty much. I wanted to help, but she did it alone."

"How big?" the kids asked.

"I can't remember exactly, but I'd say at least seventeen inches. It was the biggest of the day. Maybe the biggest of that year."

"So, she did out-fish you," Nub jabbed.

"Yeah, yeah—beginners luck."

"Who was she?" Alex probed.

"You know her."

"Huh?"

"Ahh, it was your mother."

"What?!"

"Yep, your mom fished the stream believe it or not!"

He shook his head in disbelief while Drew slugged him in the arm. Nub stretched a teeth-exposing smile. And so went another story in our family history.

Snez and I met in college a year before that trip. She wasn't a fishing person, but she bravely gave the Flag a whirl and came through with flying colors. I admired her toughness for not being accustomed to such rugged settings. Snez ended up catching more than she thought. She gave me her day back then, and in return the following year, I gave her my tomorrow with a wedding vow. I'm sure we had Gramps' blessing at the time.

The kids plunged back in their seats while Nub and I stared straight ahead. A flicker of movement had caught our eyes by the old apple orchard off to our left. Nub's foot covered the brake pedal as we neared a sharp bend in the road. Suddenly, some roadside bushes exploded with movement as we watched the back end of two white-tailed deer disappear into a collage of foliage. Their cottony tails popped up and flagged their departure as they gracefully leaped away.

"You see that?" Nub called out.

"What?" the boys responded.

"Two deer, fellas," I informed them. "Nice size too. Couldn't tell if they were bucks."

"One day we got to hunt around here. You see all the tracks by the river?" Nub asked.

"We say that every time we're here," I said in a settled voice. "We got a good thing at our deer shack and I don't see that changing."

We rolled around the bend and my focus shifted back to the road's right side. A wooded area the size of a half-dozen football fields separated us from the river.

"You see those woods?" I asked the kids. My hand swept across the scene.

"Yeah. What's the big deal?" they asked.

"Believe it or not, most of that area was a huge beaver pond back when I was in school."

"I remember walking along the backside of that thing to reach the river," Nub added.

"It's amazing how things change over time," I said. My voice drifted off as I stole a look in the rearview mirror, catching Alex's face in the background. For a moment, our images filled the reflective rectangle and I was starkly reminded of my own changes.

Nub leaned towards me and glared out my window. "Hey, is this where we hit the Hairpin Corner?" he asked while he slowed the truck.

"Jeez, I think so. It's so overgrown it's hard to tell." I looked around to sharpen my bearings. "Yeah, this is it alright."

"So, that's where you guys went in?" the kids asked. They found it hard to believe given the present day setting.

"Yep. We'd hit the river at a hole called the Hairpin Corner."

"What's with Hairpin Corner?" the kids wondered. "Where'd that name come from?"

"That's from Gramps and Pops. There's a sharp bend at that spot that reminded them of a real hairpin," I answered. "And just up from there is Ido's Stretch, named after your great grandfather because he caught so many fish there."

"Yeah, those guys had names for everybody and everything," Nub said.

"They sure did. It was funny listening to them. Hey, do you remember our family fishing at the Hairpin?" I asked.

"Barely."

"Same with me. We were all so young," I admitted. "I talked to Pops about that trip a few days ago. He said something about leaving us kids with Mom while he headed upstream. Then he sort of laughed."

The details of that trip were sketchy. We left home with four eager fishermen and an adventurous mother having piled into a '65 Chevy truck complete with a custom topper. Pops was at the helm, puffing on his pipe stuffed with Half and Half tobacco as we rolled through the Wisconsin countryside. An hour and a half later, we were stumbling along a brushy beaver dam and then through grass patches tall enough to hide a small elephant. Mom was frantic as she temporarily lost her "chicks" in the grass jungle, while Pops plowed ahead with ears pinned back and pole forward. Eventually, we all emerged from the woods and landed on a sandbank with the Flag River flowing before us. A late morning sun painted a bright picture, while a small trout splashed in front of us. A jolt of enthusiasm went through the group—and then things went downhill quick.

Our poles were a tangled mess and a bobber had flipped off along the way. We lost a ball cap on our trek and we had prickly little thorns stuck in our fingers and clothes. Mitch squirmed around and finally whispered to mom that he had to take a "number two," which got Nub and I giggling. We laughed even louder when we found out that the toilet paper hadn't made the trip. Of course that set little Mitchy off, so he flung a handful of sand at his menacing brothers, which instigated a raucous sand fight.

It took a while, but Mom and Pops settled the group and got us fishing. Pops hung around and helped with a few snags, retied a hook and put on some worms. Then, in subtle fashion, he announced that he wanted to try a few holes upstream and that he'd be right back. Mom cast a wary eye, but figured he wouldn't be far away.

After just under an hour, Pops returned to a hectic scene. Mom was at wits end and us boys were, well, being boys. An uncovered sun had made it uncomfortably warm. A pole was rendered useless thanks to a major line entanglement. Nub had soaked pant legs and Mitch complained of mosquito bites, as our bug spray had weakened and hordes of the hungry pests danced around us. All wasn't lost, however, because we caught some small trout and Pops had a few keepers in his creel. Mom was a trooper.

Those times are keepsakes, even with all the quirks, twists, and turns. Sometimes it's the haphazard, goofy times that draw people together.

27

Fishermen's Stories

I snapped back to attention as Nub jerked the wheel to avoid a darting squirrel.

"Almost hit that one," he mumbled.

I looked back but a dust cloud obscured my view. My thoughts drifted back to the Flag again. "Hey, Uncle Rocky fished these stretches too, you know."

"Yeah, I fished with him at least once," Nub replied.

"Maybe a couple of times for me. He was fun to fish with."

Although Pop's younger brother Rocky grew up in Duluth, he had left the area without navigating the Flag. His desire to pursue a teaching education took him to southern Minnesota when he was eighteen, however, he spent his college summers back in Duluth and fished the Flag with Gramps during those years. After his schooling and a work stint, he permanently migrated to California for a teaching career. Nonetheless, he continued to visit Duluth and sampled the Flag's nectar when time allowed. He was a rough and tumble type with an adventurous spirit and he fit naturally with our style of camaraderie.

It occurred to me that due to timing and circumstance, Gramps had never fished with his sons when they were young. I was an unlikely heir to that privilege. Maybe for that reason I felt like more than a grandson to him. Perhaps he lived through me, re-capturing treasured moments that were never offered with his own sons?

We couldn't mention Uncle Rocky without remembering a comical scene.

"Didn't Uncle Rocky have a friend with him one time? A funny guy," Nub asked.

"Yeah, that was Hal, the practical jokester. Actually, one time I fished with Hal, Pops and Gramps."

"Where was Uncle Rocky?"

"I don't know. He couldn't make the trip for some reason. Ole Hal pulled a fast one on me though." I shook my head with a twisted face.

"Something about a knife?"

"Yeah, a stinking knife alright. I forgot a little silver pocketknife in a sandbank from cleaning fish the week before. Well, Hal told everyone he found it in a trout he'd caught—with the blade open!"

"You believed him?" Nub half shrieked.

I paused from a mild case of humiliation. "I did. He was a good actor. And I figured the knife was small enough to look like a lure. You know, we've fished with silver spoons that are similar."

"But still, a trout would have to swallow the whole thing."

"Maybe a big enough trout could have," I weakly argued. "Anyway, Uncle Rocky finally spilled the truth years later. I heard Hal laughing across the country."

"Jeez, that's pretty bad."

The boys chuckled in the background, which encouraged me to change the subject. We passed up the gravel pit without much acknowledgement, figuring we had dwelled on it enough while driving in. We had a half-mile more of gravel road, so I dug deeper in my memory banks for more stories before parting ways with the river.

Nub beat me to the punch. "Hey, I still remember you and your buddy Steve walking up the road with a huge trout. Pops and I were at the gravel pit watching."

"Oh yeah! He got an eight-pound rainbow. The thing was so huge he couldn't land it. I climbed down the bank and shot-putted it up to him."

"Weren't you by that old snowmobile bridge?" Nub asked.

"Yep. I wonder if that wooden thing is still there. Anyway, it was too big for his creel, so we tied it onto his belt loops and boot strap and carried it that way."

"Is that the biggest trout from the Flag?" the boys asked.

"I think so, at least for our family and friends. We've all caught some big browns, but they were more in the three-to-five-pound range," I answered.

"That sounds about right," Nub agreed.

"I fished with several friends when I was in high school and college," I recalled. "That's before you and I started fishing a lot more together," I reminded Nub. "I had some good trips with Todd and Brucey—and quite a few with Rick."

"Any with your other budddies?"

I paused for a second. "Nah, I don't think so. Rob, Wade and Erickson were never here. Davis and Dahl—nope." My mind was cooking again. "Hey, do you want to hear another story?"

"Do I have a choice?" Nub dryly responded.

"Well, one time Rick and I drove here late and stayed overnight on the roadside, right around here actually. He had an old Chevy Nova—not real big. Well, at six foot tall, I didn't sleep worth a flip in that car. Plus, mosquitoes buzzed in my ear all night. Never did that again."

"At least we've gotten smarter as we've gotten older," Nub responded slyly. "Well, at least I have," he joked.

"That's debatable," I tossed back at him. "Hey, speaking of friends, maybe you should take your duck hunting buddies out here."

"Who, Al and Dave?"

"Yeah. Wouldn't they enjoy this kind of stuff?"

Nub shrugged his shoulders. "Probably so." He thought a little harder. "I'm not sure the Flag is ready for the Al and Dave show," he joked. "I'll have to pass it by them. I'm sure a trip with them would make for a few good stories!"

There's something about old fishing stories that kindles the spirit and warms the soul like a crackling fire. They can be repeated a hundred times, but they never grow old, they just grow more valuable. Great stories are often littered with half-truths and measured embellishments, but the core always stays intact, drawing attentive ears and widening smiles from every listener. They just have a way of putting you there, in the shoes of the teller, not on purpose, but more from willingness. Maybe it's because every tale reeks of hard work and adventure, and the script is written with the sweat and blood of the story's teller. Maybe it's because they're inspirational and they get the heart pumping, making even the oldest fishing buddy feel ready for another trip. Either way, every fisherman appreciates a well-told story, even if they weren't there, simply because they have dozens of their own. Those storied trips are where partnerships form and lifelong friends are made, sealing the past in a distinctive way.

We finally rolled to a stop at the crossing of Highway 13. I leaned forward and looked right, partly to check for traffic and partly to gaze towards Cranberry Creek, which was ten minutes up the road.

Nub sensed the notion and spoke about another of our trout fishing streams. "No time left to hit the Cranny, huh?"

The question's purpose was not to receive an answer, but to gin up some Cranberry Creek stories. I gladly obliged. "Nah, we're too late in the day. Hey, remember the sunbather incident?"

"Now that was something! That woman surprised the heck out of us," Nub bellowed as he turned left onto the pavement.

"Yeah, well, I think she was the most surprised of all. Especially the way she took off so fast!" I laughed.

The kids were listening and demanded an explanation. "What are you guys talking about? Some lady was in the woods sunning? That doesn't make any sense."

"Yeah, it was kind of weird, but not for her," I explained. "She'd found a sunny sandbank and was tanning I guess. It was peaceful and quiet—until we came stomping through the woods."

"She probably thought a bear was coming," Nub added. "We scared the tar out of her."

"And how about the Cranberry Inn, huh, Nub?" I asked.

"We could head there right now if you want," he laughed.

The Inn was a small place off Highway 13 in Herbster, Wisconsin, that served ice cold drinks and hot food along with a distant view of Lake Superior. Its mysterious powers lured us inside more than once, where we rested and rehashed the day amid background chatter from the locals.

Our thoughts rolled right along with the truck's wheels. "Remember our Bark River trip?" Nub asked.

"That didn't turn out too good," I said in a low voice.

The kids' finely tuned ears picked up my tone. "Hey, what river is that?" Alex asked.

"Why did you guys fish there?" Drew wondered.

"We were exploring. It's the next river past the Cranberry," I answered them. "Sometimes you have to try a new stream, you know, to have another place to go if the Flag ever goes downhill."

"Wasn't Mitch with us that time?" Nub asked.

"Yeah. We looked at a map and plowed through the woods until we found the stream."

"You guys catch anything?" Drew asked as he leaned forward.

Nub spoke and flashed a glance into the rearview mirror. "Maybe a few small ones. We never went back, I can tell you that."

"It was too sandy and shallow. Just not many holes," I recalled.

My mind changed gears when I spotted the fish boil sign at the road's edge. "Hey, check it out, Wisconsin's largest Fish Boil on Labor Day weekend—the 48th Annual, for crying out loud. Nub, we got to go one day!"

He slowed the vehicle. "I know, I know. A friend of mine said it's huge. Like hundreds and hundreds of people from all around."

"Boiled Lake Trout, potatoes and onions!"

"I imagine they have a few beers too," Nub said through a grin.

"You know, Gramps probably began fishing here when the Fish Boil started."

"Yeah, our history here is as old as the Fish Boil!" Nub said with a spark of pride. "You think he ever went?"

"Not sure. He never said. Of course, why would he tell me as a kid anyway?"

That whole scene got me thinking. Throngs of people annually gathered together for live music, a parade, arts and crafts and other activities—and of course to eat and drink. The fish, potatoes, and onions were boiled over an open fire in fresh country air. Sure the food was good, the beer went down easy, and the activities were fun, but perhaps there was a deeper purpose?

When it comes right down to it, our great country is festival crazy. Thousands of cities hold annual celebrations. My native community of Proctor holds a Hogshead Festival since it's a railroad town. South Louisiana is a festival paradise with well-known events such as Lafayette's Festival International, New Orleans' Jazz Fest, Breaux Bridge's Crawfish Festival, Rayne's Frog Festival and Abbeville's Giant Omelette Festival, where 5,000 eggs are cooked in a twelve-foot skillet.

But what's the backbone to the hoopla? Perhaps it's the underpinning of fellowship and community pride, where a people's culture and livelihood are brought to the forefront. That type of gathering keeps a person rooted to their past.

And so it was with my family, as we celebrated our ways with trips to the Flag. It wasn't a festival in the traditional sense, but the result was similar. We had our own version of food and drink, and trout fishing was our activity. We paraded through the woods instead of downtown, and our music was the river's beat. Our traditions have existed longer than some festivals, and we embraced nature and the outdoors like all good celebrations do. Our community was a close-knit family. We had fun and stayed grounded, much like the festival people.

The town of Port Wing and its Fish Boil grew a little closer to me just then. Unexpectedly, I felt tied to a festival I hadn't even attended.

28

Canvas Walls

he truck slowed and turned left, shifting my attention from the Fish Boil to the upcoming Johnson Store, complete with gas pumps and a campground. We drove into a vacated parking spot and gazed at the camping area that was off to the right in some neatly kept grass.

"Look over there guys. That's where I camped with my grandparents during our overnight trout fishing trips." I pointed with authority. "I was younger than both of you kids. It's pretty cool that people still camp there."

"It doesn't look like much," the boys said.

"Well, it's worth a pile of gold to me."

Nub added with disappointment, "I missed out on those camping trips. Gramps passed away before I was old enough to go."

"Yeah, you and Mitch got the shaft on that deal. Well, at least you have an older brother to tell the stories."

We exited the truck with that thought. I had relived the camping stories with Nub numerous times. He often listened with a child's curiosity as he attempted to enter the scene himself while I spoke.

Nub and the boys piled into the store while I wandered over to our old camping spot. It was a strange feeling, standing there. I enjoyed a moment of reflection and took myself back to an earlier time. I went on a half-dozen memorable overnight trips, with one in particular standing out when I was eleven years old.

After Gramps and I spent a day fishing the lower portion of the Flag, we drove back to their screened canvas camper. That's where Grandma worked her magic, making us feel at home. After a change of clothes, I took my place alongside the kitchen table and found a spot on the soft foam bench. I was in a comfortable stupor as fresh volumes of north woods air pressed against the camper screen. Sunlight sliced through the camper as the setting sun eased its grip over the peaceful town of Port Wing. A lone car on Highway 13 drifted past us in near silence amid a background chorus of chirping crickets. Grandma stayed busy before me in the kitchen. Gramps stayed busy behind me outdoors. All was right with the world.

After we wolfed down a delicious meal that featured fresh fried trout, Grandma reached for two decks of cards and Gramps went back outside and finished the prep work for tomorrow's fishing.

"Tony, are you ready for a few games of double solitaire?" she asked.

"Of course Grams, I was wondering if you still wanted to play after I beat you last time," I answered in a playful way.

"Oh, I don't think I remember that," she jokingly replied.

The mood suddenly became a bit more serious when the game commenced. After all, this was a showdown for the championship of the camper. The game was challenging because each person could play off the other's cards at the top of the spread. A player received one point for each card they played at the top, and lost one point for each card that wasn't turned over on their own side. We usually played to one hundred points, which required playing multiple games.

We had entered the early stages of battle when the game's pace started to get the best of Grandma. I noticed the telltale signs from past experience. Her coarse, salt and peppered hair began to shake and her hands quivered like Edith Bunker on *All in the Family*. A pair of thick lenses in gold-rimmed frames couldn't hide a concerned expression.

"Tony!" she shrieked in Edith Bunker style. "What are you doing here?"

"I'm on a good run, Grams," I mumbled while keeping my eyes on the game.

"Well, you need to slow down a bit," she complained.

"Or maybe you need to speed up a bit," I joked.

I slapped another card on the top row.

"You know Grams, I don't remember you slowing down when you're winning."

Silence followed as she finally played some cards on the top row and turned another over from her side stack. Her hands moved with surprising quickness.

"Huh, what was that?" she asked.

"Oh nothing," I giggled. "Let's just keep playing."

I was getting the best of Grandma again when midway through the contest she made an unprecedented move, one that might be considered a breach of double solitaire etiquette. While I shuffled the deck for another game, she went and uncovered a fresh baked apple pie and placed it beside me. Her apple pie was my all-time favorite.

"Tony, that's for after the game," she said while shuffling her own deck.

What could I say? It looked delicious, and then the aroma of apples and cinnamon smacked me in the nose like a prizefighter. I almost staggered while sitting.

Needless to say, I was mildly distracted for the remainder of the match and she came back for a rousing victory. Afterwards, she served me the biggest piece of pie ever. Somehow we both came out winners that evening.

Gramps entered the camper after the commotion settled and we discussed a plan for the next day's fishing while Grandma finished cleaning the dishes.

He stood over me as I devoured my piece of pie. "So how's my big trout fisherman doing?"

"Pretty good, Gramps," I said while wiping off some crumbs. "I'm kind of pooped out though."

"Why?" he said as he leaned over. "After all, I caught all the trout today," he said with a hearty chuckle.

"Hey, wait a minute!"

"I'm just kidding. You did great today."

I looked at him to make sure he was joking around. His approval was my blue ribbon.

"You caught your share today, grandson. You're starting to get it," he assured me.

I sensed a hint of pride in his voice.

"What stretch should we fish tomorrow morning, Gramps?"

He methodically stepped across the camper before answering. "How about we try The Logjam stretch? We'll start at the Hairpin Corner and fish up from there."

"Are there a lot of good holes?" I asked while putting my paper plate in the garbage.

"Plenty. We might even run into one of them big browns."

"Good. I can't wait!"

A burst of adrenaline kept me going to help Grandma finish cleaning up.

Shortly afterwards, I piled into an inviting sleeping bag and nestled my nose in the pillow. Everything smelled fresher out there. I rolled over and glimpsed the sun's last vestige as it set fire to a jagged skyline. Numerous mosquitoes clung to the small rectangular mesh window alongside my bed and stared at me, while others softly bounced off it.

"Sorry dudes, you're not biting me tonight," I whispered while flicking the mesh a few times, sending the winged wisps floating away. A breath of outdoor scent touched my face and settled around me. I was as content as a front porch hound dog on a lazy summer day. Life was good. I felt loved.

My brother called out from the store's entrance and demanded my attention. "Hey, are you coming in? There's a lot of smoked fish in the back."

"Yeah, I'm coming—just walking around our old camping spot thinking about the good ole days."

He slipped back in the store and I hurried behind him. It was a small place, as a shopper could stroll through the aisles in a few minutes, but it held all the essentials, including some specialty foods. Most importantly, however, was the country store's serene setting and warm atmosphere.

I didn't get but two steps past the front door, when a smiling young lady at the cash register extended me a greeting. "Hi! Welcome, and come on in," she said.

"Hey there, how are you doing?"

"Just fine, thank you," she said politely.

My eyes shifted past her and stopped at the back wall, where a refrigerated section cooled the locally caught, smoked fish. I resisted the urge to head back there, and instead followed Nub and walked the aisles searching for some picnic items. The kids, in the meantime, were glued to the candy section as they sniffed around for their favorite treats.

"What do you think, Nubby?"

He slowed and squinted at the chest-high shelves. "I found the Wheat Thins. That's what we usually get, right?"

"I think so. They go good with the smoked fish." I moistened my lips thinking about the meal ahead. "What else do we need?"

Nub's hand slid to his hip as he paused in thought. "Some paper plates, plastic forks, and maybe some napkins."

"Oh, and let's get some Adolph's Meat Tenderizer for Alex's wasp sting. It reduces the swelling," I said.

"Really? Well, let's give it a try," Nub responded.

We found our items in short order and sauntered over to the refrigerated section. Lord have mercy we hit the gold mine. Everett's Smoked Fish labels were slapped across a variety of fish types, including whitefish, herring, ciscoes, lake trout, and our favorite, the brown sugar-cured salmon. We grabbed some salmon, ciscoes, and a pack of Wisconsin cheese curds for good measure.

Everett Johnson comes from a long line of commercial fishermen. In the 1940s, Everett began smoking the fish they caught, and they've been at it ever since, perfecting their technique, making a mouth-watering product.

We called the boys over for their viewing pleasure before we headed to the counter. They poked at the bronze clad fish with curiosity. A few minutes later our friendly attendant rang up the tab, bagged our groceries, and sent us on our way. We made a paste from the meat tenderizer and covered Alex's swollen wasp bite. It relieved him in short order.

Before we turned back onto Highway 13, a humorous story needed telling.

"Hey, Uncle Rocky camped over there too, "I said while pointing at the grounds.

"Not sure I knew that," Nub responded.

The boys were half listening thanks to a new loot of candy.

"Anyway, he was with Gramps, Rizzy, and another friend. He said it was the most miserable night in his life," I said while trying to contain my laughter.

Nub looked a bit perplexed.

"Yeah, he couldn't sleep at all, so he left the camper and slept in a car." I paused for the explanation. "Rocky said it was so loud from the snoring, burping and farting that he didn't have a chance. He said the air was moving so much that the camper sides looked like they were breathing!"

Nub and I roared in laughter. I turned back and caught some smirks lining the kid's faces. A few seconds later, the giggles got the best of them.

29

Wayside Our Style

*W*e exited the parking lot on a high note and reunited with the paved carpet of Highway 13. I stole a glance through the rearview mirror and watched the last shapes of Port Wing fade into the distance. I preferred seeing the town through the front windshield, but it was a soothing sight nonetheless.

The boys seemed content in the back seat as they nibbled on their Sour Skittles and Fun-Dips. Nub was equally at ease as he drove, with one hand resting softly on the wheel. His expression was more relaxed now than it was earlier. It's interesting what a great day on the stream does to a person.

Undoubtedly, a good day on the stream improved one's mood; however, a history of good days improved one's life. I felt blessed to have experienced both.

I rolled up my window and cut down the road noise.

"Well Nub, we did a good job planning the day out."

"Like how do you mean? We only planned to fish."

"That's exactly what I mean," I said triumphantly. "What did Gramps always say when he went fishing?"

"Oh yeah, he said something like—keep the ends open. Like, don't plan anything else during a fishing trip."

"You got it!"

That was good advice we lived by. By design, there weren't any schedules when we fished, which kept stress levels to a minimum.

The day's adventures dictated when we got home, which was usually early evening.

We sped down the highway, catching glimpses of Lake Superior between breaks in a strip of forest that lined the lakeshore. Up next on our agenda was picnicking at the wayside rest area with the scenic overlook. Five minutes later, we were there.

"There she is," Nubby exclaimed as he slowed and turned right into the looped parking lot.

"Looks like it did forty years ago," I pointed out.

We parked and carried the cooler over to our favorite wooden table and unloaded our goodies. The kids wandered over to a hand pump, and after several strokes, breathed life into its metal body as cold water gushed out the bottom. The squeaky pump caught our attention, so we paused for a warm look. The kids moved around and grinned amid the splashing water.

"That was us a long time ago, eh Nub?"

"Yeah, it was," he said after a long swallow of beer.

"Hey you two," I hollered. "Come on back and eat."

They stumbled towards us full of smiles, exchanging friendly shoves along the way. They both had water stains scattered across their t-shirts, and Alex's pant leg was wet.

"What were you guys doing over there?" I asked, pretending to be aggravated.

"Looks like you two were in a water balloon fight," Nub added. "And you both lost."

"I stood in front of the well and Drew started pumping like crazy," Alex explained. "Then water shot out the bottom and got me."

Drew cracked up as Alex replayed the scene. "I thought it worked like that. I just wasn't sure any water would come out," Drew laughed.

Nub and I admired the playful jousting between our sons.

We all sat and dug into the spread before us, which included a jar of pickled green beans straight from Nub's garden.

"Wow, these babies are good!" I expressed after gobbling up a bean.

"That's from last year's canning," Nub informed us. "We had a bumper crop."

Pointed shadows were cast over our table thanks to some pine tops intercepting the sun's rays. The kids chomped on the fish, popped a few cheese curds in their mouth, and slurped on their root beers. We ate in silence for a few minutes, occasionally shooing away some annoying flies. Fortunately, the lake breeze was strong enough to whisk away the lightweight mosquitoes.

"It's weird to think that as kids we ate lunches here with Gramps and Pops," I said to Nub.

"And how about the "pizza pie" that Gramps made, huh? That was good stuff."

"Yeah, I liked that a lot, except for the onions," I replied.

The kids lifted their eyes looking for an explanation, so I followed through. "Gramps made a dish he called pizza pie for every fishing trip. He put eggs, salami, pepperoni, cheese, onions from his garden, and garlic in an aluminum pan. He salted and peppered it good." My hands shaped a plate-sized sphere over the table as I spoke. "He cooked it either on the stove or in the oven. It came out great each time. We ate it with some bread and chips."

Both Nub and I had tried duplicating Gramps' authentic recipe, but for some reason our versions didn't quite taste the same. That was a typical result for anybody trying to match their grandparents' cooking. It was one of life's great mysteries.

As I removed the backbone from the salmon, a chunk of fish flew away to the ground.

"Dang it," I said, staring at the piece in the grass. "Well, that's the way the pickle squirts!"

"Huh?" the kids responded.

I laughed. "That was another of Gramps' sayings. It meant that's the way things go—you know, stuff happens unexpectedly. Like when you bite a pickle, sometimes juice squirts out and surprises you."

"Are you making that up?" the boys asked in disbelief.

Nub backed me up. "No, I remember that. We didn't hear it much, but I remember it."

"That's weird," they said.

"Come on, it's kind of cool in its own sort of way," I responded.

Our eating pace slowed as we filled up, which resulted in the boys venturing off towards the rock throwing spot under some tall pines. A minute later they disappeared down a steep, dirt bank that led to the lake. We cleaned the table and headed to the bluff, where we watched the kids skip rocks across the lake's surface.

"There's another thing we used to do," Nub said as he pointed towards the boys. "And we even tried swimming a few times, but it's too dang cold."

"You got that right. I won't be jumping in there anytime soon."

With that thought, I lifted my eyes and scanned across Lake Superior's great expanse, straining to see the other side. It's an amazing feature about the size of South Carolina, claiming rights as the largest freshwater lake in the world by surface area. It's nearly 160 miles wide at its widest point. Lake Superior has always been held in high regard by its nearby inhabitants, including the Ojibwe, who called it Gichigami, meaning "great sea."

The view from our perch backed the Ojibwe's thoughts. Sunshine angled off the lake's broad chest, while shrugs from its massive shoulders sent shimmering rays in all directions. A freshwater smell brought the lake inside of me and gave me a lift. Puffs of clouds blew over the spectacular scene, as if they were winded from the Almighty's nostrils. I took a deep breath and felt myself grow to match the vision.

I sensed some irony while looking outward, for earlier I had felt small under a majestic black spruce, but now I felt big over the giant lake. Nature works in mysterious ways. Sometimes it's best to enjoy the ride and rationalize later.

Nub's bark startled me as he called the boys. "Hey, you guys, come back up."

While they scrambled up the bank, we kicked around and looked for choice throwing stones. A top-flight stone not only had good weight and shape, but it felt balanced in the hand. Rock selection could make or break a competition. Unfortunately, for some of us, we needed a rock shot from a cannon for victory.

Nub and I rotated our arms while the boys, slightly out of breath, joined us with the loot of rocks they found on the shore. They reluctantly "borrowed" us a few upon our request, which came with the threats of WWF headlocks if they didn't comply.

"Well, Nubby, how about you go first?" I encouraged.

"Yeah, Uncle Nub can't throw anyway, so let's get him out of the way," Alex teased.

"Hey, I played third base for a long time until I hurt my rotator cuff," he reminded us.

"Okay rifle arm, show us what you got," I said.

What happened next was an athletic lowlight in Dincau family history, as my brother's geriatric attempt sent a rock barely far enough to hit water. A painful grunt resonated away from his flailing body.

"What the heck was that?" I asked. "That was a horrible throw and it looked even worse."

"The ole arm's a little stiff," Nub said while rubbing his shoulder.

I took center stage and did better, but not enough to prevent the kids from snickering.

"Alright, Drew, it's time to show your stuff," I said.

He stepped up and gave a good effort as the rock sailed high and landed deep, leaving pulsating rings that were erased by the lake's incoming waves. That toss put him in first place.

"Alright Alex, you're up," Nub directed.

"Yeah, don't trip or anything," Drew said as he gave him a friendly shove.

Alex took a pitcher's wind up and his left arm smoothly flung the rock to the farthest distance yet. He strutted around with a concealed smile.

We all took a few more attempts, but in the end, Alex was the champion—again.

"How many times have I won now?" Alex asked. "Maybe the last four in a row?"

"Something like that," I responded. "But hey, Nub and I have bad shoulders, and Drew is younger than you." I looked over the lake for a second. "How about this, Mr. Champ? Try throwing to that huge boulder sticking out of the water."

Alex took a good look at the challenge. "How much will you give me?"

The massive boulder was at least ten yards past his farthest throw, so I wasn't too worried. "How about twenty bucks?"

"Nah, how about fifty?"

"What? You think I'm made of gold?"

Nub and Drew chuckled in the background.

"Fine, fifty bucks, but it can't be an inch short."

Alex took his time and found the perfect rock. With a determined look, he hopped forward, stretched his arm back and sent the stone to its new residence—right alongside the boulder.

"Wow, look at that!" Nub shouted.

Drew laughed at me as I dug into my wallet.

"Jeez, Loueeze," I lamented while slapping the bills in Alex's hand.

He stayed silent, but he carried a look of the cat that ate the canary.

We headed towards our picnic table as echoes from our family fun drifted off and were consumed by a shoreline of lapping waves. A constant breeze pushed against our backs as we carried our goods back to the truck. I took a last look around, catching sight of the water pump, the picnic table, our rock throwing perch, and of course, the lake. Sometimes it's the simple places that stay with us.

30

A Child's Wonder

*H*ighway 13 treated us right on the way home, offering soothing country views without much traffic. The boys were quiet except for an occasional slurp of pop, while Nub and I exchanged intermittent chatter. We dropped into the shaded Brule River Valley without much discussion, as all our trout fishing energy had been spent. We climbed up the other side and then rode through several miles of sunny pastures.

I let out a humorous sigh after catching sight of some feeding cows.

Nub took notice. "What was that for?"

I hesitated to answer. "Ahh, a joke crossed my mind. It's not very funny, but there's some history to it."

As expected, Nub went on high alert. "Like what do you mean?"

"Well, the day I fished with Gramps, Pops, and Hal, we drove down this stretch of road and Hal asked me if I knew the easiest way to count the number of cows in a field." I took a short breath. "I told him to count them one by one. Hal said no, no Tony, just count the legs and divide by four!"

"That's the joke?" Nub asked.

"Yep. I didn't find it funny at the time and I still don't. But Pops burst out laughing. He thought it was the funniest thing. He still brings it up once in a while."

"Man, that's weak. Maybe Pops needs to get out a little more often," Nub chuckled.

We continued our trek westward towards a sinking sun. A smoothly paved road combined with the truck's monotonous hum nearly had me dozing off when Nub's voice sparked conversation.

"How long do you figure Gramps fished the Flag?" he asked.

"Well, maybe twenty years or so." I held a thoughtful stare out the window. "Actually, Pops fished about twenty years himself up until he couldn't see good enough to retie hooks."

Nub's head nudged back. "And you fished there for how long? Maybe thirty-five years?"

"Wow! I didn't think about it that way."

"Yeah, you've been there about as long as Gramps and Pops combined," Nub reiterated. "You were the main person that taught me about the Flag."

"Really?"

"Yeah. I was too young to fish much with Gramps. I fished some with Pops and even a few times by myself. After Pops stopped going, we started fishing together more often, and it's been that way ever since."

I was flabbergasted. "That doesn't seem right, but I guess so."

Nub filled in some more gaps. "You fished a lot with your friends after Gramps passed away. And then when I was about seventeen I became your full-time partner."

"I remember that," I said with warmth. "You finally got old enough where you weren't a pain in the rear. You really liked going."

"I remember us catching our limit of ten back then," Nub pointed out. "Only that eight of the fish were yours and only two were mine!"

"You were a bit rusty coming out of the gate," I recalled.

"And then you'd catch fish behind me, right after I'd fished a hole. Man that pissed me off. I remember thinking, what am I doing wrong?"

"Well, I had a lot more teaching from Gramps and Pops," I said.

"It took me about ten years with you, but I finally caught up. I remember a few times I even caught a few more than you."

"Hey, watch it pal, before I charge you for my services!" I joked.

"Anyway, while Gramps and Pops got me going, you locked me in. I wouldn't be on these trips now if it weren't for you."

A strange feeling permeated my body. For years I'd focused on the ways of my mentors, not recognizing that long ago I had stepped into that role myself. I mused over the fact the I was the "old man" on the stream, the one with the history, the stories, the one that hopefully my family looked up to. It was a good feeling.

The kids perked up as we left Highway 13 and headed north towards Superior, Wisconsin.

"Are we going straight home?" they asked.

"Yeah," I responded.

Their question had an underlying reason. We occasionally detoured through Gary-New Duluth and brought my wife's Grandfather Stevo and Aunt Desa a few trout for dinner. However, Stevo was nearly a hundred years old and his taste for trout had waned, plus we were tired and the day had drawn long.

That question stirred up some history that I felt compelled to share with the kids. "You know, after your great grandpa passed away in 1979, I brought trout to your great grandma for years. And they lived less than a mile from your great grandpa Stevo as it turned out. I've been bringing trout to our family in Gary for a long time."

In the distance, geometric shapes from Superior's city limits punctured the horizon, which prompted another thought.

"When I fished with Gramps, we used to come through Superior from that direction," I said, while pointing left.

"You mean from the west, like through Oliver?" Nub asked for clarification.

"Yeah, it was a shorter route from his house. We drove through Oliver, then by the Calvary Cemetery, then along the Nemadji Golf Course, and finally we popped out on the south side of Superior."

Nub stirred in his seat. "We need to do that one day!"

The "old" route into Superior had some special meaning. While the small town of Oliver now rested quietly, it was a rip-roaring place over fifty years ago. It attracted a reveling crowd, which included the likes of my father, grandfather, and many other relatives on both my father and mother's side. Also, many of my dad's further removed relatives, none of whom I ever met, lived in the country outskirts of Oliver. A drive through town left me wondering about the past.

The Calvary Cemetery houses many of my relatives, including my trout-fishing grandparents. It's likely that my own parents may take residence there one day. The cemetery is carved from a pine-studded hillside that overlooks the meandering Pokegama River, which oddly enough, resembles the Lower Flag River. The same Lake Superior red clay that cradles the Flag River also encases all who are buried at Calvary. There is a mystical connection between the two places for our family.

We worked our way through Superior, crossed over the St. Louis River, and headed up the steep hill back to Proctor, Minnesota. A short time later, Nub guided the truck alongside our parents' house and parked it under the familiar shadow of a giant silver maple that anchored the yard's corner. The old, two-story house was our childhood home, and it was soothing to end our trip at its doorstep.

While we stretched our legs outside the truck, our families poured from the house. Our girls took the lead and ran towards us like a litter of puppies. Snez and Chris hustled behind their children, while Mom followed with her normal peppy step. Pops was last in line and not to be rushed. Their presence raised our spirits, and the light fragrance of cooling August air helped make a happy scene.

"Where's the fish?" Amanda asked. Her big browns eyes glowed as she waited for the answer.

I moved towards the truck bed while Nub dropped the tailgate. "Back here," I said. I grabbed a bag of fish from the cooler. "Look at these beauties!"

Ice water dripped from the bag's corner and splattered on the ground.

Mandi poked at the fish through the bag. "Yuck!" she exclaimed. "They look all slimy." Wisps of blonde hair dashed across her face as she pulled away.

We opened the bag and Nicole fiddled with a trout's lower jaw. "Where's their teeth?" she asked. "I don't see anything in their mouth but a little white tongue looking thing." Her ponytail bobbed around as she waited for an explanation.

Before we could answer, Amanda chimed in. "Do they still have their guts in?" she asked.

"Nah," Nub replied. "We cleaned them at the stream."

"Those look like some nice ones!" Chris said.

"But they're still smaller than the one I caught," Snez joked.

I rolled my eyes. "Oh, boy, here we go again."

Mom stepped beside us guys and gave us all a hug. "How are my big fishermen? Did you guys have a great time?"

"One of the best trips we ever had," I told her with a smile.

"Where did you guys fish?" Pops asked.

"We hit the left fork, Pops. They were really biting today," I answered.

"Did you get down by the Logjam or the Hairpin?" Pops asked with an arched eyebrow.

I knew that was coming. Pops' line of questioning had become somewhat predictable since he retired from the stream years ago.

"Nah, we didn't have enough time. Plus, we limited out anyway," I justified to him.

"We're due for another visit down there," Nub chimed in. "We'll hit it next time."

Pops grabbed the bag of fish and scanned them over. "You got some brookies in here, huh?"

"Yeah," Nub answered. "Most of them are brookies."

In a loud voice, Pops piped up. "A brook-a-trout! A brook-a-trout!"

The girls giggled and the boys sported confused grins.

"What's that name?" Alex and Drew asked as they grabbed a half-dozen trout from the bag for a pending picture.

Cousins and Their Catch

I laughed. "That's just another one of Pops' nicknames."

I stepped to the cooler and pulled out a second bag.

"Here's the rest of our haul," I announced as everyone looked on.

"How do you want to split these up?" I asked Nub.

"How about we leave a few here and I'll smoke the rest? I smoked a few last year and they were real good," Nub emphasized.

I turned towards my parents. "How about we sauté the rest of these in butter, onion, and garlic and splash some lemon juice on them."

"Yeah, I like them like that," Pops said as he smacked his lips.

Mom agreed through a beaming smile.

And so it was, four fishermen were embraced by their families after a day on the stream. It embodied who we were.

As the group mingled, Mom made an announcement. "There's homemade manicotti baking in the oven," she said with a bright smile. "And there might be a fresh baked apple pie hanging around!"

That information sent the group into an uproar. As we recollected ourselves, I leaned over the truck and stared at our equipment for the last time today.

"You want to take everything back to your house?" I asked Nub.

"Yeah, I'll put it all in the pole barn."

The rods and vests were to be put back in a quiet corner, the hip boots were to be turned inside out to dry, and the creels and worm cans were to be hung in the breeze. That was standard operating procedure.

"Well, Drew and I are heading out," Nub said as he closed the tailgate. "We'll be back to eat after we clean up and put the stuff away."

"Sounds like a plan," I said. "I'm heading inside to shower."

Fifteen minutes later I walked upstairs from the basement shower and paused over a sunlit dining room table that was dressed for dinner. I heard the kids frolicking and the adults talking outside on the lawn. I wanted to join the fray but the day's efforts had taken its toll, and I became defenseless as a nearby recliner drew me into its lap. My mind wandered as I rested. I couldn't help but reflect on the day's trip and on our history of trips.

There is a powerful force that draws a trout fisherman back to his stream, and it goes well beyond the catch. It's about the solemn walk to the first trout hole, the enjoyment of a streamside lunch, the day's recall while cleaning fish, and the feeling of having family and friends around an overnight campfire.

Through our many pilgrimages, I better understand why a salmon swims up the same stream from which it originated. The sights, sounds, scent, and feel of the environment are unique, not to be duplicated anywhere else. These elements forge the memories of trips gone by, and slowly become woven into the fiber of one's body, mind and soul.

Four generations of fishing tradition pumped through my body as surely as the pulse in my veins. I was not only a lucky trout fisherman, but also a lucky man.

Beyond that, I was a drowsy man trying to stay conscious. A few adults entered the kitchen and rattled some dishes. Their voices seemed muffled because I wasn't coherent. I fought to become alert again, to become fully awakened.

And then, as all good dreams must end, I finally did awaken to a comfortably similar setting.

31

Passing the Torch

*D*rifting back into consciousness can be a sullen feeling, especially after a wonderful ride with the Dreamweaver. Back in Louisiana, my eyes crack open to a remote resting on my chest; it hadn't budged since I nodded off. *Gunsmoke* no longer occupies my screen. To my comfort, warm smells and soft sounds emanate from the kitchen as my family mingles before dinner.

Thoughts of our Flag River trips have me lazily grinning. Those resonating adventures helped me become a better person and taught me the value of positive role models. Our outings encourage family togetherness and offer one-on-one time unmatched in any other setting. It provides a means for my grandfather to hold hands with his great grandchildren, linking the most distant generations.

Perhaps life isn't so puzzling when you find a sense of belonging, when you find a place that's helps you find yourself—a place where you grow up being taught strong values, and then grow old teaching the same to the next generation. Sometimes it takes a brush with mortality to recognize those places, where your perspective on life becomes clear.

I chuckle while heading towards the dinner table. Somehow a trout fishing dream turned into a soulful event, where fishermen and nature became one, and where our family grew closer together. I'm a fortunate man indeed, and I'm deeply thankful for the time my forefathers spent with me. In doing so, they showed me that the greatest gift one human can give to another is heartfelt time, where true togetherness is born from desire versus duty.

Five Reasons to Give Thanks

As my family gathers at the dinner table, I take a good look at my wife Snez, my son Alex, and my daughters Amanda and Nicole. While this may be just another dinner to them, it isn't for me, not after that nap. My experiences on the stream help me visualize the important role I play in keeping my family together. As we join hands to give thanks, I more clearly understand the value of this simple moment, one that hopefully my children will share often with their future families, thereby passing the torch.

Perhaps the soul of a trout fisherman goes much deeper than the holes he fishes?

Uncle Nub's Smoked Trout

10 fresh stream trout, cleaned, with tails and head on
1 gallon of fresh water
1 cup of brown sugar
7/8 cup of pickling salt
¼ gallon of fresh cut, native to your area maple and alder wood chips
Olive oil for basting

Directions:

Mix sugar and salt in a gallon of fresh water until dissolved to make brine. Separately, soak wood chips in water for 20 minutes before use. Refrigerate fish in brine for 12 hours and then pat dry with paper towels. Grease racks and trout with olive oil using Pampered Chef Oil Sprayer. Smoke at 150 degrees for 1 hour and 20 minutes and then 160 degrees for 1 hour and 30 minutes. Let trout cool at least 1 hour before eating. Enjoy with a side of Wisconsin cheese curds and crackers. Delicioso!

Cousin's Campfire Trout

5 fresh stream trout, cleaned, with tails and head on or off
Salt and pepper
2 tablespoons of minced garlic cloves
1 small sweet onion, cubed
½ stick of butter
½ fresh cut lemon
3 tablespoons of chopped fresh parsley
4 tablespoons of olive oil
Reynold's aluminum foil

Directions:

Rinse fish in cold water and pat dry with a paper towel. Sauté onion and garlic in a lightly oiled pan for 5 minutes to soften. Add onion and garlic mix, and slices of butter to inside and outside of fish. Drizzle olive oil on fish, salt and pepper to taste, and double wrap with foil. Place fish under a medium campfire near hot embers for about 15 minutes, depending on heat intensity. Remove when fish is cooked through. Place fish on a platter and squeeze on lemon juice to taste, and sprinkle with parsley. Enjoy with Italian bread and a glass of white wine. Mangiare!

– For sautéed trout in a pan, melt butter with olive oil and add onion and garlic, and then 5 minutes later add fish dusted with flour. Salt and pepper to taste while flipping fish when brown. Squeeze on fresh lemon juice and sprinkle with parsley before transferring to a serving plate.

Printed in the United States
By Bookmasters